DWARF
FRUIT TREES
For Home Gardens

I.B. LUCAS

DOVER PUBLICATIONS, INC.
NEW YORK

NOTE TO THE DOVER EDITION

SINCE the original edition of this book appeared in 1946, new developments in both pesticide research and environmental legislation have brought many changes in the areas of plant spraying and pest control. The reader is advised to consult his County Agricultural Agent or State Extension Service for the latest recommendations. In addition, information concerning the specific available varieties of dwarf fruits may have been affected by the introduction of new strains. Contact local growers and nurseries for information concerning the latest varieties recommended for use in your area.

Published in Canada by General Publishing Company, Ltd., 30 Lesmill Road, Don Mills, Toronto, Ontario.

Published in the United Kingdom by Constable and Company, Ltd., 10 Orange Street, London WC2H 7EG.

This Dover edition, first published in 1977, is an unabridged republication of the work published by A. T. De La Mare Company, Inc., New York, in 1946.

International Standard Book Number: 0-486-23530-0
Library of Congress Catalog Card Number: 77-76874

Manufactured in the United States of America
Dover Publications, Inc.
180 Varick Street
New York, N.Y. 10014

CONTENTS

ILLUSTRATIONS

INTRODUCTION

THIS IS my story of dwarf fruit trees and their superiority over the old-fashioned standard fruit trees. It will show what is possible in any sunny back yard, no matter how small. While it opens up a whole new world of garden pleasures it also names the terms on which you may succeed with them. The terms are easy: You must prune, cultivate, fertilize, and dust according to instructions; if you would grow Peaches beyond their usual northerly limits you must protect them.

There are two reasons why any reader who follows the instructions is sure to succeed. The first is: My own garden is in a locality in which almost every condition is unfavourable for growing fruit. Markdale, Ontario, Canada has a very short Summer, is remote from any temperature-equalizing body of water and so is subject to terrific late frosts following unseasonable warm spells, and within the past ten years my thermograph has recorded two dips of 40 deg. below zero. Even the soil is wrong for this climate. It is a heavy clay loam and retards ripening. And yet, by observing the rules, I have had no difficulty in growing to perfection a representative assortment of all the familiar pome and stone fruits. Moreover, my conclusions are based not on a few coddled specimens but on nearly a thousand trees which, incidentally, occupy slightly less than an acre.

The second reason is that from time to time I have set forth in my cabin trailer on a tour of gardens where dwarfs have been planted. In this way I found out what mistakes were most commonly made and what advice needed special emphasis. "Pruning instructions," one man told me, "are perfectly simple when I study them in a book but very confusing when I find myself face to face with a tree requiring pruning." I have accordingly taken great pains to tell just how to prune. I have even tested my advice on a number of inquirers. They, too, have made helpful suggestions.

I learned other things on these tours, apart from my discovery that garden-lovers are perfectly delightful and hospitable people. For instance, I sometimes found a gardener busily engaged doing all the wrong things to his trees but doing them thoroughly and with enthusiasm. For him I predict success and ultimate joy in his trees. Any gardener who is really interested in dwarf trees can learn a great deal about their needs by observing them closely. To save time and disappointment, instruction and observation should go hand in hand.

The dwarf tree is of particular interest to the owner of the very small garden, since he has space for nothing larger, but it should be of almost equal value to the owner of more extensive premises. It would be a very large estate indeed which could boast a domestic orchard of standard trees bearing a well balanced assortment of the most desirable varieties of Apples, Pears, Peaches, Apricots, Nectarines, Plums and Cherries. But this is quite feasible with small trees. For instance, a row of ten single cordons planted a foot and a half apart along a wire fence 15 feet long will provide one of each of the outstanding Apple types—and they will ripen in succession. The same is true of Pears. The stone fruits do not lend themselves to cordon training and thus occupy a little more space. Trained as fans or in bush form, it would be easy to have a representative collection of varieties of all the stone fruits in any good-sized garden.

It is to be hoped, however, that the reader will temper his enthusiasm for immediately establishing an extensive garden of dwarf fruit trees. To succeed he must give his trees careful and regular attention. He should make a modest start with only a few trees and enlarge his planting in keeping with his success and interest. In conclusion, it is to be hoped that this book may be the means of launching him in a form of fruit culture which, given half a chance, will add beauty and charm to his garden from blossom time until harvest and provide his table with all kinds of luscious, mellow-ripe fruit.

A FORM WELL ADAPTED FOR APPLES, PEARS, OR PLUMS. TWO OR THREE PAIRS MAKE A NOVEL AND EFFECTIVE ARCH OVER A GATEWAY

Chapter 1

WHY YOU WILL WANT TO GROW DWARF FRUIT

He does the Savage Hawthorn teach
To bear the Medlar and the Pear
He bids the rustic Plum to rear
A noble trunk and be a Peach
Ev'n Daphne's* coyness he does mock,
And weds the Cherry to her stock,
Though she refused Apollo's suit;
Ev'n she, that chaste and Virgin Tree,
Now wonders at herself, to see
That she's a Mother made, and blushes in her Fruit.
—Abraham Cowley, *1688*.

A CULTIVATED fruit tree is never grown on its own roots. It is composed of two parts, the root (stock or rootstock) and the cion. The rootstock is a small seedling, or it may be a rooted sucker, from a tree which if allowed to mature would, in most cases, produce worthless fruit. Its sole merit lies in its roots which, when propagated as rootstocks and budded or grafted with buds or cions from a tree bearing fruit of the desired variety, imparts to the resulting tree certain characters such as vigor or hardiness.

BUDDING A ROOTSTOCK

A one or two year old seedling or rooted sucker is used for this purpose. In late July or early August (for Apples) a T cut is made in the bark of the rootstock

*Daphne, loved by Apollo, escaped his amorous attentions by being changed into a laurel.

3 or 4 inches above the ground and the cion or shield bud, A, is inserted as shown in AA and wrapped with a rubber band. The following Spring, before growth starts, the rootstock is cut off leaving a stub, B, and during that growing season the one-year-old whip or maiden, AAA, develops. (See Fig. 1.)

Next March the stub B is removed and by Fall the scar has partly healed as shown in concluding diagram.

A dwarf fruit tree might be described as one grown on a rootstock which dwarfs it. But, because almost all fruit varieties when grown on roots other than their own are thereby made smaller, that definition would hardly do. The fact is that the term is loosely applied by pomologists to any fruit tree which, in their opinion, has been reduced in size by the influence of its rootstock to such a marked degree as to warrant its being so described. It appears therefore that there is no clear line of demarcation between dwarfs and standards and that such terms, in this connection, are merely descriptive. Thus, trees that are not quite small enough to be classed as dwarfs are said to be weak-growing; those a little larger are variously described as moderately vigorous, vigorous, or very vigorous.

The term, dwarf fruit tree, embraces all the pome (Pear, Apple, and Quince) and stone fruits and includes trees on rootstocks of widely different character and vigor, therefore any generalizations regarding them can hardly be strictly accurate. Nevertheless, there is a surprising degree of uniformity in the character and needs of all kinds which have been dwarfed to an equal degree.

By the use of the Malling IX Apple rootstock we can grow any variety of Apple as an extreme dwarf. But not every fruit has a successful, dwarfing rootstock within its botanical family circle corresponding to the Malling IX for Apples. Therefore, where the rootstock we are using does not sufficiently dwarf our tree we have to adopt other methods to limit its growth such as (1)

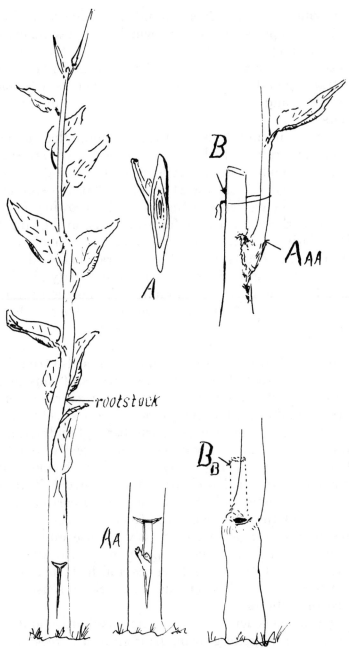

FIG. 1. BUDDING A ROOTSTOCK

removing branches which extend the framework of the tree (2) repressive pruning, which includes pinching, root-pruning, and Summer-pruning (3) the various methods of restricting growth discussed under the topic of training and (4) cultural practices such as withholding food and water and restricting or confining the roots.

The subject of dwarf fruit trees is unfamiliar to most people and riddled with misconceptions. Here are three rather sweeping but, we believe, accurate statements: (1) in every way the dwarf is better than the standard for the home garden (2) the advice for growing dwarfs is not identical with that for standards, and owing to the relative smallness of the trees it is much more simple (3) contrary to the general belief dwarfs, instead of being confined to the more southerly districts, have been the means of extending the northerly limits of the different fruits far beyond anything hitherto thought possible. The idea that they are less hardy may be due to the fact that the Quince roots on which Pears are dwarfed are rather tender. It is also true that all dwarfing roots tend to be shallower and thus more exposed to dangerous freezing. Under average home garden conditions, however, root tenderness seldom results in losses because fences, shrubberies, buildings, and other windbreaks usually prevent the protective blanket of snow from blowing away as it does in the more exposed commercial orchards. In any event it takes only a few moments to throw a mound of earth against the base of the tree before the freeze-up. As an absolute guarantee against root injury a loose mulch may be added but this should be postponed until after the freeze-up and the mice have established themselves elsewhere in their Winter quarters. (See discussion of mice and rabbits.)

Let us consider the fascinating possibilities and the many advantages of growing fruit on dwarf trees in the home garden.

1. *Dusting.* In the average home garden it is difficult to either dust or spray the big old fashioned standard trees. Under normal conditions dwarfs can be adequately protected by the use of a combination, all-purpose, fungicide-insecticide dust. The nuisance of mastering the intricate spray calendars for the different fruits and measuring and weighing the minute quantities required for half a dozen trees has no doubt caused many an amateur to abandon the idea of growing his own fruit. The use of an all-purpose dust involves none of this messiness or nuisance or study and it can be applied at odd moments without preparation. Spray, as applied by the amateur, frequently fails to protect the plants from the pests. Sometimes this is due to under-concentration. Or it may be due to over-concentration which results in burning the foliage, especially when it has been mistakenly applied on too-tender foliage, or at the wrong period. Dust, on the other hand, can be applied with absolute safety subject only to a few simple and obvious qualifications dealt with in a later chapter.

2. *Quick Bearing.* Some Apples purchased as two-year-olds will set fruit the year they are planted. This indicates how extremely precocious is the Apple dwarfed on Malling IX. Unfortunately, it also indicates that the tree was not pruned severely enough in the nursery. A tree that has been properly pruned in the nursery, and subsequently in the garden, will not set fruit before its second, and preferably not before its third year in the garden. This breathing spell enables the tree to establish itself after the shock of transplanting and gives it an opportunity to develop a sturdy framework and the stamina to stand up under the strain of the very heavy fruit bearing which is characteristic of Apples on this rootstock. We should not begrudge it this extra year or two because it will still be in full bearing years ahead of the corresponding varie-

ties grown as standards. It will be six or seven years ahead in the case of the Northern Spy. The other fruits as dwarfs have the same tendency toward early bearing but because they begin to bear quite early as full-sized trees, this advantage is not so important as in the case of Apples.

3. *Peaches at* 40 *Deg. Below Zero.* If you live north of the so-called Peach Belt and have resigned yourself to relying on market Peaches of uncertain quality you may be interested to know that, with very little attention, you can grow in your own garden fancy-quality Peaches to eat "out of hand" and that your only dependence on market Peaches will be for canning for which purpose they will be satisfactory. So also with Apricots, Nectarines, and the less hardy varieties of dessert Pears, Sweet Cherries, and Plums. This is due partly to dwarfing stocks which are at the same time hardier than Peach roots (that is, the Plum stocks on which Peaches are dwarfed), and partly due to the ease with which dwarfs may be protected by windbreaks, wrapping, and covers.

4. *Succession Throughout Season.* One of the absurdities often seen in the home garden is a huge tree of Summer Apples, the Yellow Transparent for example, which during its brief harvest may produce a surplus of perhaps 29 Apples for every one that can be used by the family. Of these 29 a few may be given away to the neighbors but they are more likely to be gathered up and buried to avoid attracting flies. Since they will not keep for more than a few days after picking, this superabundance is followed by an Apple famine. With dwarfs as many as nine different varieties of all kinds of Summer fruits could be grown in the space occupied by that Yellow Transparent thus providing a succession of all kinds of fruit with only sufficient for the family needs at any one time.

5. *Quality and Size of Fruit.* **Pears** grown on Quince are definitely larger, Apples are certainly as large and in my opinion slightly larger, and every kind of fruit grown as a dwarf produces sweeter, better-colored, better-flavored and earlier-maturing fruit. In England and the Continent dwarfs are used to grow the fancy or extra-quality fruit known as "Tray Fruits," the term being derived from the trays in which the street vendors carry their fruit.

6. *Care Is More Convenient.* Anyone who has tried to wield a cumbersome pruning tool while perched 15 or 20 feet above the ground with one foot painfully wedged in a crotch and the other braced against a branch of uncertain strength will regard this heading as a masterpiece of understatement. We appreciate what a luxury it is to be able to prune, spray, thin, and pick while both feet remain firmly and comfortably planted on the ground.

7. *Transplanting.* Dwarfs may be transplanted successfully at any age due to their relatively small size and the fibrous nature of their roots. In fact it is not uncommon, so I have heard, for the English tenant to move his small orchard of dwarfs along with him from place to place. Obviously each transplanting, even with dwarfs, checks growth and, if possible, should be avoided, especially with older trees.

8. *Shallow Rooting.* This makes possible the growing of fruit on land that has not sufficient depth for standards. Their shallow root system leaves them more liable to uprooting (in the case of Apples) and so for this reason, and also because of weakness at or below the union in several cion and stock combinations, staking is sometimes necessary.

9. *Garden Crops Possible.* Since they are so small and low and because their roots usually do not extend far beyond the spread of their branches, they do not

shade or interfere with the growth of vegetables planted close to them. When trained on walls they, of course, throw no shade at all.

10. *Control of Biennial Bearing.* Dwarfs are more prolific than standards and while this takes its toll by shortening their life the difference in the initial cost is negligible over the period of from 20 to 30 years that a dwarf Apple, for example, may be expected to produce profitably. Any tendency toward biennial bearing can very readily be controlled owing to the ease with which the operations of disbudding or thinning out the blossoms or newly-set fruit can be carried out.

11. *Ornamental.* There are few garden plants that can approach in ornamental value a fan-trained Amsden June Peach in full bloom or bearing its burden of mellow-ripe fruit. If such a specimen is trained against a weathered brick wall—well, we won't attempt to describe it but it is the ultimate in something. The other fruits trained as espaliers or even as single cordons are likewise most attractive.

DISADVANTAGES

We have said that in every way the dwarf is more suitable than the standard for the home garden. We have also said that their care, though simpler, is different and involves a few practices which are not required in caring for standards. In that sense these practices might be regarded as disadvantages and, though far outweighed by the advantages, they should perhaps be listed.

1. Staking is necessary in some cases. (See planting.)

2. They require protection from rabbits and mice longer than standards.

3. In the Spring the snow, beneath which the dwarfs may be more or less buried, has a tendency in some sea-

sons to form a crust which adheres firmly to the branches pulling them down and breaking them as the drifts subside. In order to guard against this form of injury it is sometimes necessary to tie in toward the center of the tree any horizontal branches which might otherwise be broken off. When thus tied in, it is a simple matter to prevent this damage. Merely break the crust in a ring around the tree so that the tree is only required to support the weight of a small amount of crust. The snow, however, is not altogether evil, for it affords a large measure of protection against dangerous low temperatures.

4. Apples on Malling IX tend to come into bearing too early and to overbear. To counteract these tendencies it is necessary to (1) cultivate intensively (2) fertilize heavily and mulch and (3) prune for wood growth rather than for fruit. See subsequent chapters for detailed directions.

Chapter 2

DWARFING ROOTSTOCKS

THE AMATEUR who has purchased a couple of dwarfs, or even several dozen, is probably not concerned with the story of how these miniature types were developed. Nevertheless, it is important that he should know on what rootstocks his trees are growing. Not so long ago this might have presented considerable difficulty since there used to be great confusion as to the exact identification of rootstocks for fruit trees, particularly apple rootstocks. Now, thanks to the work of the East Malling Research Station in Kent, England, these have been clearly distinguished and identified. Malling classifications are accepted as standard throughout the world.

Is It Important to Know Your Rootstocks? Let us take an example. A Peach is often dwarfed on a Saint Julien C rootstock. As this is a Plum stock you have to decide whether the soil, moisture, drainage, and fertility are suitable for growing Plums—not Peaches. Let us take another example. There is only one satisfactory dwarfing rootstock for the Apple, the Malling IX Apple rootstock, and in the average garden that grows good vegetables it will develop into a healthy dwarf that might reach 10 feet high but could readily be checked at 4 feet. In loose, gravelly, or sandy soil that dries out badly in Summer or in soil that lacks fertility growth will come almost to a standstill and the tree may die. In that case you will be obliged to take as second choice the more vigorous Malling IV or the even more vigorous Malling II Apple rootstock (also called

Doucin) which has relatively coarse, deep roots that can reach sources of moisture and which under adverse conditions, such as above described, would nevertheless make a moderate growth. But only under the foregoing extreme circumstances should Malling II be considered, it will produce a tree in the normal garden which is not much smaller than the old-fashioned standard.

The beginner should carefully note the name of the rootstock used for each tree he buys, and should obtain from his nurseryman instructions as to its needs. The character and cultural needs of Malling IX used for Apples are dealt with in the Apple chapter; and the Quince stock used for Pears is similarly discussed in the Pear chapter. But there is such a wide range of rootstocks in use for dwarfing the stone fruits that it is not feasible to do likewise for them.

Before leaving the subject of rootstocks it is interesting, and perhaps not without practical value, to consider briefly the ways in which a rootstock dwarfs the cion variety (or clon) budded or grafted on it and in what other ways the performance of a variety is influenced by its rootstock.

Why Do We Use Rootstocks? A rootstock is a tree of the same botanical family as the cion on to which, a few inches above the ground, the desired fruit variety (*i.e.* cion) is budded. Such a bud then forms the head, and the rootstock plant is cut off immediately above. The fruit variety could be propagated vegetatively (that is, on its own roots) but the use of selected rootstocks is preferable for the following reasons: (1) earlier bearing (2) hardiness (3) ability to dwarf or increase the size (4) tolerance of special soil conditions, acidity, or alkalinity, or of excessively moist or dry soil (5) resistance to disease or insects. Such rootstocks may be increased vegetatively by cuttings or suckers. In this case it is said to be a clonal rootstock and possesses the identical character of the parent; or it may be grown from seed in which case there may be more or less variation in seedlings even from the same tree.

What Is a Variety? Almost every named fruit, the McIntosh Apple for example, is descended from one original seed. If seeds from a McIntosh should be planted some of the resulting fruit might resemble the McIntosh but the vast majority of them would not. A bud from a McIntosh is inserted in a suitable rootstock if we desire a true McIntosh Apple. A plant that does not "come true" from seed but must be reproduced vegetatively by budding or grafting or by rooting suckers or cuttings is said to be a clon. All Apple and Pear varieties are clons and so also, with rare exceptions, are the stone fruit varieties.

By What Means Does a Rootstock Influence Growth? Science has not settled this question yet. Many theories suggest themselves but cases refute them. It used to be said that the dwarfing effect of a rootstock was due to its inability to supply water and soil nutrients to the top. Unfortunately, for this theory, it appears that certain Apple stocks and cion varieties grow more vigorously when grafted together than either does on its own roots.

What Are the Qualities of a Good Rootstock? We have been mainly concerned thus far with the ability of a rootstock to dwarf the cion but a rootstock must pass a number of other tests before it can be pronounced satisfactory. Is the resulting tree reasonably long-lived is it healthy, is it fruitful? Is the rootstock itself healthy, resistant to disease and pests (nematodes, borers and the root aphis, for example), tolerant of a wide range of soil and moisture conditions? Can it be propagated readily in the nursery?

The near-perfect dwarfing rootstock for Apples has been found in Malling IX; and for Pears the clonal Quince rootstocks, Malling A (Angers), B, and C, though totally incompatible with certain varieties and unsatisfactory for others, are satisfactory for a long list of good varieties.

In the case of the stone fruits there is nothing corresponding to the Malling IX which is compatible with all kinds of Apples. The Saint Julien C Plum rootstock, for instance, is excellent for Peaches, Apricots, and some Plums but is very difficult to increase in the nursery. The Sand Cherries are too dwarfing, and so on. In the meantime research stations throughout the world are constantly searching for something better and—such is the skill of the modern plant scientist—usually finding it.

In a recent review of the world literature on the subject of rootstocks for dwarfing the stone fruits, the author commented on the results of all recorded experimental trials; the different combinations tested for Peaches numbered 81, for Apricots 34, for Cherries 80, and for Plums no less than 396. It will be seen, therefore, that there is nothing final about the list that follows.

DWARFING ROOTSTOCKS FOR PLUMS

Native or American Plum Seedlings (*Prunus americana*). The native wild Plums are compatible with the cultivated American varieties and have a moderately dwarfing effect. European and Japanese varieties are dwarfed but, by commercial standards, are not sufficiently compatible because the trees are too short-lived and the union is rather weak. There should be little danger of breakage in home gardens if the tree is staked and headed low to avoid undue leverage.

Sand Cherry Seedlings (*Prunus pumila*). This is the Sand Cherry, not to be confused with Prunus besseyi, the Western Sand Cherry. It is said to dwarf the Americana varieties but is not favorably regarded by present experimenters.

Bessey or Western Sand Cherry Seedlings (*Prunus besseyi*). This is apparently a satisfactory stock for Japanese Plums in general. In 1906 Professor N. E. Hansen reported that he had found all varieties of the species *Prunus domestica* uncongenial and short-lived and that the union was not durable. Notwithstanding this adverse judgment, numerous tests have again been undertaken with all the Plum species and it is hoped that combinations that were previously condemned by the criterion of their performance in commercial orchards may at least be found suitable for home gardens.

Saint Julien Plum (*Prunus insititia*). The clonal strain known as Saint Julien C (Malling classification) has been found satisfactory for Domestica Plums in general but is unfortunately very slow to multiply in the nursery. Consequently nearly all these stocks are raised from seed and are very variable. Trees worked on them show wide differences in compatibility, growth, strength of union, and cropping. Seedling stocks of Saint Julien should therefore be avoided.

DWARFING ROOTSTOCKS FOR PEACHES

Saint Julien Plum (*Prunus insititia*). See discussion of this rootstock in the preceding paragraph. The clonal strain, Saint Julien C, I have found ideal for Peaches. It produces healthy trees of just the right vigor for fan-training. "Mother" rows, with the protection of a foot of snow, have survived 40 deg. below zero in my garden. It is said that it will succeed in a wide range of soil and moisture conditions. Peaches worked on this clon (a clon is a plant that does not come true to seed) in my garden came into bearing in a very short time. For example, Amsden June Peaches in their first growing season grew from the original cion bud into small fans, produced some bloom the next year, and a sample of fruit in their third growing year. The following year they were loaded with fruit and had to be severely thinned. This was not true of some other identical specimens. My soil, a clay loam, does not lend itself to early maturity and in a warmer, lighter soil the preco- cious bearing above-described should be the rule.

Bessey or Western Sand Cherry (*Prunus besseyi*). See under Plum Stocks. It is recommended as an ex- tremely dwarfing, but healthy, stock for all varieties of Peaches. It is pointed out that it requires budding early in the season. Unlike the Saint Julien stock it has the advantage of reproducing itself by seed with no appre- ciable variation.

Beach Plum (*Prunus maritima*). This is the shrubby Plum found growing in the hot sands along the Atlantic seashore. In the only reported case in which this Plum was used as a stock for Peaches (several varieties were tested) it was adjudged worthless: "buds made good growth until midseason, then all died out within two to three weeks." This trial took place in Iowa. Fortunately Mr. Alfred Reoch, at that time Superintendent of the S. Z. Mitchell Estate on Long Island, had not heard of these failures and budded a considerable number of Peaches of different varieties on stocks grown from seeds of this shrub that he had gathered along the beach. When he showed them to me they were, I be- lieve, about eight or ten years old and were healthy, medium dwarfed specimens. Mr. Reoch had found them completely compatible up to that time, fruitful, and apparently they had just the right vigor for wall training or as bushes for the home garden. I tried grow- ing some seed but whether they were too tender, or needed a light soil, or possibly were just pining for the smell of the salt spray, they failed to flourish and now, at the beginning of their third growing season, the seed- lings are still too slender for budding. If this digression on the subject of the Beach Plum is rather inconclusive it at least indicates the need for further research and suggests how the amateur can help by testing the root-stock-cion combinations which have shown promise at the government research stations.

DWARFING ROOTSTOCKS FOR APRICOTS

Much uncertainty exists as to dwarfing stocks for Apricots. East Malling recommends Saint Julien C but although I tried a few and had 60 per cent of the buds take I subsequently lost these trees, as two-year-olds, due to Autumn transplanting followed by a Winter with 40 deg. below zero temperatures. Our native Plum, *Prunus americana,* is a satisfactory rootstock for Apricots and makes a good union with it but although moderate in growth, it is hardly a dwarfing rootstock. Apricot on *Prunus americana* which in turn had been worked on *Prunus besseyi* should produce, in theory at least, a thrifty dwarf. *Prunus besseyi* is described by Hansen in 1904 as "apparently satisfactory as a dwarfing stock for Apricots" but even now there still seems to be no satisfactory reported evidence on its long range performance.

ROOTSTOCKS FOR CHERRIES

Of the two stocks at present being used in this country for all kinds of Cherries, namely Mazzard and Mahaleb, the latter has a slightly dwarfing effect. A much more dwarfed tree will result from the use of the Sour Cherry stocks, Kentish and Stockton Morello (*Prunus cerasus*), but these are not generally available in this country at present. On Stockton Morello there is a very great overgrowth at the union but the union itself is nevertheless strong. Bailey considers that *P. pumila* and *P. besseyi* both show promise as dwarfing stocks but Hansen states that Cherries, whether sweet or sour, will unite with the latter only with difficulty whether budded or grafted.

N. B. A rootstock not discussed in this chapter is Saint Julien A. I have never worked with it or even seen it but all reports indicate that it is identical with Saint Julien C in its rootstock effects. There was therefore nothing to be gained by dealing with it separately.

Chapter 3

PLANNING AND PLANTING

In planning our garden of dwarf fruit trees for some years to come we will not have the wide choice of varieties that is available in Europe. Literally thousands of varieties from all over the world have been tried out in this country by the various fruit-testing associations and government agencies but the tests are invariably: will they ship, will they keep, have they display value, are they productive, in short are they profitable? These are the fruits that the industry demands and that nurserymen stock and it is from these that the home owner must make his selection.

By some law of compensation the tender-skinned, luscious fruit is never a good shipper. And there is an almost mathematical precision in the way dessert quality is bred out as keeping quality is bred in. When, after years of selection and breeding, the plant breeder triumphantly produces the perfect keeper he is dismayed to find that its quality has receded to a point where there ceases to be any virtue in keeping it. I hasten to add that there are some notable exceptions to this law in the case of certain Apples and Pears but very rarely in the stone fruits. The law of compensations is equally in evidence in the matter of productiveness. The Doyenne du Comice is reputed to be our finest Pear but is very shy-bearing and quite temperamental about bearing at all. At the bottom of the list, in order of quality, is the Kieffer Pear—"this whited sepulcher of a fruit" as M. G. Kains scornfully calls it—

and, in accordance with this law, no other Pear can approach it for fruitfulness.

Apples, Pears, Plums and Cherries have been dealt with in four separate chapters. Peaches, Nectarines and Apricots, due to their comparatively similar cultural needs, have been discussed in a fifth chapter. Each chapter concludes with a discussion of varieties and their special uses and in these chapters the all-important question of pollination is also covered.

Few suburban dwellers have a flat, sunny, rectangular lot suitably located south of the dwelling and favored with a deep, well-drained, sweet soil of the type that grows good vegetables. Too many gardens are located at the north end of the lot and are so hemmed in by buildings and by shrubberries and trees with their overhanging foliage and encroaching roots that the successful growing of fruit is out of the question. If you lack experience with fruit you should have some qualified person look over your site and check on your soil before embarking on the discouraging, nay hopeless, job of establishing a fruit garden under such unfavorable conditions.

Shallow Planting. We have inspected many hundreds of dwarf trees and have yet to find a grower who does not, in our opinion, plant Apple trees too deeply.* We are almost tempted to propound the theory that a grower's experience with Apples is in inverse proportion to the depth he plants his Apples. At least we found that our own education with them conformed to this thesis for each year found us planting shallower than the preceding one. Our insistence on shallow planting being based on our experiments in our own garden soil, a fairly rich, well-drained, clay loam, we cannot speak with quite the same conviction with regard to different conditions. It would seem, however,

---

*Throughout this text it is understood that apples are dwarfed on Malling IX and pears are dwarfed on Quince A, B, or C.

that this advice would apply with even greater force in the case of heavy clays, especially if not well-drained, whereas light or sandy soil would indicate considerably deeper planting. But when in doubt, plant shallow, in fact, without doubt, plant very shallow.

Evil of Cion Rooting. In most Apples the union between the cion and rootstock is only a few inches above the roots. If the soil comes in contact with this union there is a tendency for the cion to throw out its own roots. When this happens the tree soon ceases to be a dwarf either in size or character. The dwarfing rootstock no longer influences the tree in any way and often dies. It is not sufficient to allow a margin of merely 1 or 2 inches because soil does a surprising amount of shifting about, especially on a slope. Applications of manure and mulches build it up. Pears also will cion-root but not so readily as Apples.

The illustration, Fig. 3, indicates the correct planting depth for Apples on Malling IX. It also shows the approved method of staking. Apples require staking for the twofold reason that (1) although the union is strong the rootstock is extremely brittle and the roots may break off a few inches out from the base of the tree and (2) the entire root system, being shallow, may be uprooted.

The Quince rootstock on which the Pear is dwarfed is just the opposite. Its roots are strong and firmly anchored but its union with the less compatible varieties of Pears is very weak.

In a sheltered location Apples that are not over 5 or 6 feet high and which have been headed not more than about a foot above the ground need not be staked but Pears that are listed as less than "completely compatible with Quince" should always be staked.

Staking. The stakes should be sturdy and preferably of Cedar. If you are planting a considerable number of trees we would suggest light Cedar poles as they can be obtained very cheaply in most districts and, if treated with some preservative such as creosote in a green shade, will last almost indefinitely and be quite inconspicuous. Whatever sort of stake is used there should be no bark left on it as it would provide a refuge for insects. The stake may be set in first and the tree planted against it in which case it should be vertical. However, when transplanting an older tree to a different position in your garden we find it more convenient to drive the stake afterwards at an angle so that it will not disturb the ball of earth moved with the roots.

When both tree and stake are in position the tree should be tied to the stake with some soft, light rope in such a way that, as the soil settles and the tree sinks lower, it will not become "hung" but will settle naturally. This will take about six months. The tie should then be adjusted and made permanent. This permanent tie may again be a strong, soft rope but if it is soft it will necessarily not last very long. A much better tie is made with a Willow wand (Salix caprea). It should last for three years, cannot possibly injure the bark by rubbing or girdling, and it holds the tree more firmly than any other tie. These Willows can be obtained from your nursery where they are used to tie up bundles of nursery stock. Or you can cut them yourself in almost any swamp. If you intend to train some of your trees you should grow a clump or two in your garden. They are ideal for screening a compost heap or any unsightly spot. There is a peculiar satisfaction in working with Willow wands. Try it and see if you don't agree.

Correcting Too Vigorous Roots. The Malling IX roots are, if anything, a little too weak-growing and we must try to promote the most vigorous growth possible. The Pear dwarfed on Quince C is slightly more vigorous, and on Quince A and B it is much more vigorous. There is much variation in the relative vigor of Quince A, B and C in different soils. This is true also of the rootstocks used for dwarfing the stone fruits. Thus where a rootstock is inclined to be too vigorous for our purpose we must adopt a number of practices for checking it and the first step in this direction should be taken when planting. In order to proceed intelligently we should understand the underlying principles involved. Dealing with the subject in a broad general way it might be said at the outset that the root system of any tree consists of roots whose main function is to supply water and which are called taproots. Others which supply food are fibrous or feeding roots. Actually there is no such simple or sharp distinction. The taproots tend to be large, with few laterals. They penetrate deeply into the soil and at a fairly sharp angle. In direct proportion with these characteristics the tree will be large, vigorous, slow to come into bearing, shy-bearing when it does come in and, in short, less like a dwarf and more like a standard. It follows as an immediate corollary to this statement that the fibrous roots have the opposite tendency and are the ones to be encouraged. In the extreme case of heavy roots going almost straight down, it is necessary to remove them entirely, but where they can be bent gently upwards and spread out near the surface, this less Spartan treatment is to be preferred as the taproot in this position loses its power to force the tree into too vigorous growth and yet the health or life of the tree has not been endangered.

I tried another method with gratifying results. In a wide shallow hole, when planting, I incorporated a considerable amount of very fibrous, moisture-retaining material such as peatmoss, leafmold, and old manure. A couple of years later these materials were found to have become filled with fibrous roots with a corresponding decrease in production of taproots and the desirable characteristics above indicated were the result.

Planting in Containers. Fruit trees that have no rootstocks which sufficiently dwarf the trees may be

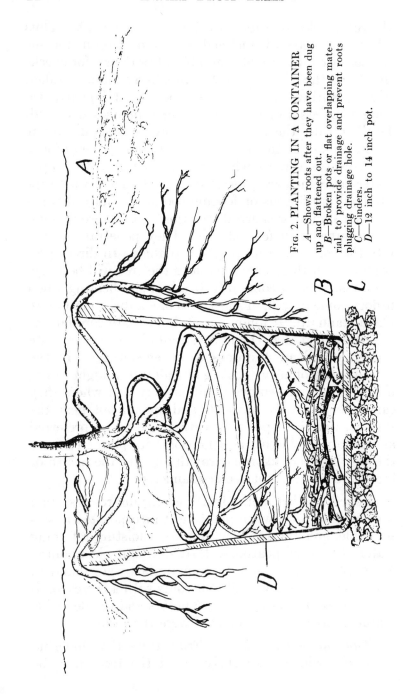

Fig. 2. PLANTING IN A CONTAINER

A—Shows roots after they have been dug up and flattened out.

B—Broken pots or flat overlapping material, to provide drainage and prevent roots plugging drainage hole.

C—Cinders.

D—12 inch to 14 inch pot.

planted in some container which is then sunk in the ground so that its rim is at or just below the surface. It remains permanently in the ground and its function is to confine the taproots. The result is that the taproots drawn by the more plentiful moisture at the bottom of the container may never escape over the edge or top but remain permanently imprisoned. Incidentally, the greatest care should be taken to see that there is a thick layer of broken flower pots covering the drainage hole to prevent the roots finding and plugging it. The fibrous or fine surface-feeding roots, on the other hand, readily flow over the sides. In time some of these escaping roots will grow downwards and develop into taproots and unless lifted and flattened out close to the surface will induce strong growth. If deemed advisable, this is a simple matter. In the meantime the tree should now be producing a crop and unwanted growth can be more easily controlled. With these broad general principles in mind we are ready for planting.

How to Plant. Prepare the ground in readiness for the tree a month or more before Fall planting. For Spring planting prepare in the Fall. This consists of removing the soil to a depth of about a foot but not deeper than the subsoil if it is gravel or pure clay. Drainage material is placed in the bottom and most of the soil is then replaced, stamping it firmly from time to time as it is added if the tree is to be planted immediately. If the soil is rather dry it will be impossible to tramp it too firmly. But never stamp soil that is moist enough to cake, especially if there is much clay in it. Plant 2 to 3 inches higher if a tree is planted on top of a foot of freshly worked soil that is too moist to tramp firmly. Under these adverse conditions you will have to rely on rain or, as second choice, artificial watering to settle the soil. Mulching of newly planted trees is always desirable but is absolutely essential under these conditions. Staking may also be necessary if the soil is too wet to be firmed. In fact, temporary staking is always an advantage with newly planted trees.

We have not used the expression "dig a hole" since it is too suggestive of the post-hole-like excavations we have so often observed. For Apples the shallow depression in which the tree is finally planted is not more than 4 to 5 inches deep and at least wide enough to permit the roots to be spread out radially to their full length without bending. If your labor is not a consideration, a margin of 6 to 8 inches beyond the reach of the roots would be a definite advantage. Other dwarfs should be planted at the same depth as in nursery.

After placing the tree in position prepared soil to a depth of 6 to 7 inches should be added, thus raising it 2 inches above the surrounding soil. To your garden soil add an equal amount of organic matter. This might consist of equal parts of peatmoss, wellrotted manure, and half-decayed hardwood leaves. A pound of bonemeal and a quart or two of charcoal will help.

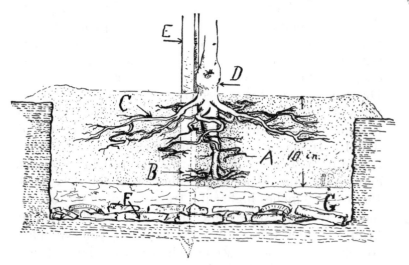

FIG. 3. HOW TO PLANT AN APPLE ON MALLING IX

A—Prepared soil; B—Original roots; C—Most vigorous roots placed very close to the surface; D—Union between stock and cion well above the soil; E—Stake; F—Drainage material; G—Surface soil thrown back on top of drainage material.

The foregoing instructions might be criticised as being a counsel of perfection and we not only agree but quite frankly confess that it has to be a mighty valuable tree before we will take that much trouble with it. Moreover, the growing of fruit trees is far from being one of the exact sciences and the mixture just described is little more than a rough guess based partly on one person's intuition and partly on standard horticultural practice. For instance, instead of the three organic ingredients it might prove in practice under your particular conditions of soil and moisture that a preponderance or the exclusive use of one might be preferable. You might need peatmoss on account of its greater capacity for holding moisture, or manure because of a lack of fertility in the surrounding soil. Leafmold combines to a lesser degree the advantages of the other two and was suggested because it is usually available wherever there is a garden. And so, with an understanding of the purpose for which these ingredients are used, an interested gardener can adapt, improvise, and vary the specific instructions to suit local conditions.

It is desirable to at least cover the roots with the same prepared soil as that on which they are planted. If the soil is in a good friable condition it will not be necessary to spend time working it into the open spaces beneath the trunk. By firming the soil well around the outer roots with your feet to within 10 to 12 inches of the trunk, meanwhile jigging the tree up and down, enough soil will work into these spaces to protect them temporarily. The soil that is later placed around the tree will soon be carried down into these spaces by the rain if kept in a loose condition by cultivation or a mulch. If staked there is again less need to firm the soil close to the base of the tree. Fig. 3 shows this operation much more accurately than it can be described.

If planting in the Fall soil should be mounded up around the trunk about a foot and extended well out over the root spread. It should be made slightly higher and firmer immediately next to the trunk. If left too loose, the Fall rains may wash some soil away from the trunk leaving a space which may fill with ice and injure the bark. Mounding should be done as late as possible in the Fall. If done too early, the base of the trunk covered by the soil will be more tender than the exposed portion, and as the soil subsides with the Fall rains a collar of tender bark will be exposed which may be winterkilled. In the Spring this mound is removed and a mulch applied.

For Spring planting a different method is followed. The surface should be slightly dished so that the rain will penetrate the soil instead of running away. In addition there should be a mulch 2 or 3 inches thick over the entire root run. This may consist of any material that will prevent the moisture escaping. Decayed leaves, strawy manure, or straw are all satisfactory. This mulch should be drawn aside occasionally to permit shallow cultivation. The following Spring this material may be incorporated with the soil.

The use of manure at planting time is subject to some qualifications. If fresh, it should be mixed with the subsoil and then covered with at least 4 inches of soil that is free of manure. If old, well-decayed manure is used, it should be thoroughly incorporated with the soil which is in contact with the roots and since the roots usually come from the nursery with no soil it may be as well to omit the manure from the soil around or above the roots. It has the paradoxical effect of increasing the moisture content of the soil while at the same time drying the roots. In fact, the only fertilizer that can be safely added when planting is bonemeal since its action is very slow and you might use several times the indicated amount with no harmful effects.

Pruning When Planting. With Apples the pruning of one-year-old whips (maidens as they are called in England) is delayed till the early Spring if Fall-planted but is done immediately if Spring-planted. But it is usual to buy two-year-olds. Varieties that are slow to come into bearing such as McIntosh or Delicious may be headed as high as 18 inches but all quick-bearing varieties should be headed (as maidens) at not more than 12 inches above the ground if you hope to prevent premature bearing. If your nursery heads them too high it will pay you to buy one-year-olds and head them yourself. Prune Apples or Pears intended as cordons only to shorten laterals if any (see Spurring).

Pear maiden may be headed back as directed for Apples but being less precocious in the matter of early bearing (except on Quince C) they should not be headed back so severely.

The problem cannot be disposed of so easily in the case of the stone fruits. We have to consider whether a tree is on an extreme dwarfing rootstock, or a rather too vigorous one. If you wish to obtain maximum size you should prune the newly-planted trees as little as possible consistent with the ability of its roots to support it through its first critical Summer. How little that should be depends on (1) the condition of the roots (2) the type of soil and (3) that unknown quantity, the weather. In commercial orchards where maximum growth is always sought the English, with moist, moderate Summers, omit pruning when planting, whereas California, with dry Summers, prunes when planting. They are both right for their local environmental conditions. To check growth, merely reverse this rule.

In the case of Apples we are always trying for maximum vigor and were it not for its tendency to start right in developing fruit buds instead of a framework (Fig. 7) our advice would be the same as for the weak-growing types of stone fruits. But instead, we must prune to get growth buds.

Chapter 4

CONTROL OF INSECTS, DISEASES, AND ANIMAL PESTS

EFFECTIVE control of insects, fungi, and diseases is a *sine qua non* of fruit growing. By substituting an all-purpose dust for liquid sprays we have eliminated at one fell swoop all the intricate entomological, chemical, pharmaceutical, physiological, botanical and even mechanical problems involved in the use of the familiar "Spray Calendars" issued by government or other agencies. In other words, it is because there is not a great deal that an amateur needs to know about such a dust or its use. If it is applied regularly and frequently, preferably before rainy or foggy weather, during the first three growing months it will afford a reasonable measure of protection in the case of dwarfs in home gardens.

Whatever may be the relative merits of sprays and dusts in commercial orchards or on large trees there can be no need in a small garden for the study and labor involved in digesting the complicated spray instructions—each succeeding spray being modified and each kind of fruit having its own quite different set of requirements.

Advantages of Dusting. Dust, unlike spray, may be left in your dust gun, or rotary-type duster, without the dust deteriorating and without the duster becoming corroded. Your duster should hang in some cool, dry, convenient place ready for instant use when you go for a stroll in your garden. There is no changing of clothes, no tiresome measuring of minute quantities of caustic or poisonous chemicals, no need to throw away the unused balance, or to wash the equipment to prevent corrosion, or to guard against injury to foliage due to applying spray that is too strong, or applying it at the wrong time, or too often, or allowing caustic Apple sprays to drift over on tender Peach leaves. There are many other points in favor of dust but space is limited and the gardener has at least been put on his inquiry.

Of What Is This All-Purpose Dust Composed? The answer to this question will probably change frequently in the years to come and recommendations for one district will have to be modified to adapt them to the different conditions in others. The requirements of such a dust are that it must be sufficiently non-caustic so that it will not injure Peach foliage; it will contain a stomach poison which will be unnecessary in the earliest sprays but will be present when needed and it will probably contain one of the sulphur fungicides. For aphids, the plant lice found on the undersides of terminal leaves, use any of the contact dusts—rotenone, derris, or nicotine sulphate. These may be used either separately or added to your all-purpose dust.

In the absence of an all-purpose dust especially designed for fruit trees the dust used in commercial orchards for Peaches, the one which includes dusting sulphur and lead arsenate, will be found satisfactory. It is much cheaper than the all-purpose dusts sold for Roses and just as effective for your purpose. If the smallest commercial package of the above Peach dust (sulphur plus lead arsenate) is more than you can use in one season you can keep it over until the following year with no appreciable deterioration provided it is kept cool and perfectly dry. The other dusts, rotenone, derris, and nicotine sulphate, lose their strength fairly quickly and should not be kept from one season to the next and should always be kept cool and in air-tight containers. Do not forget that sulphur may injure foliage during very hot weather.

When and How Is It Applied? That is a question that can best be answered by some local fruit grower or your State Research Station. They will know what pests are most troublesome in your territory. There may even be some that can only be held in check by one of the dormant sprays. If so you may be able to borrow the necessary spray equipment for that single dormant application.

On the other hand, you may learn that certain fruits may require little or no dust in your district. North of the Peach Belt Peaches are often completely free of diseases and insect injury. Plums are often without any disease or insect except the Plum curculio which, so far as I know, is always present. Many varieties of Pears are very free from trouble and so are sour Cherries. Apples always need plenty of dust, roughly about every ten days during the first three growing months. Using it before periods of wet weather, even in the midst of several days of rain, is more important than applying it at regular intervals. Still air and dewy mornings facilitate dusting.

Mice

In commercial orchards mounding of soil 6 inches or 8 inches against the base of young trees is frequently relied on to prevent mouse damage. While mounding seems to be very satisfactory many gardeners may have more confidence in a wire guard: wrap the trunk with a piece of coarse galvanized 1/4-inch mesh wire 12 inches to 18 inches high and whatever width is necessary to encircle the trunk and allow for five or six years' growth. Tramping the snow close to the trunk after each snowfall will have the same effect as mounding; mice always work along or near the ground underneath the snow and will detour around any such obstruction. For the same reason a path in the snow around a group of trees will form an effective guard against mice. Sometimes a hard crust is covered with a later snowfall and on occasion mice will work along it. But I have never observed them working on such a crust higher than 10 inches or 12 inches above the ground.

Materials suitable as Winter mulches against frost are unfortunately suitable as nests for mice and should not be applied until after the ground is frozen solid by which time the mice have established their nests elsewhere. Mounding with soil should also be delayed as long as possible since that part of the trunk covered with soil remains more tender and when the mound subsides with the Fall rains it leaves a ring of tender bark that is likely to be injured by Winter frosts.

Probably the best poison bait for mice is strychnine-grains. Mix 1 level tablespoonful of laundry starch in $\frac{1}{4}$ cup of cold water. Stir this into $\frac{3}{4}$ pint of boiling water to make a clear paste. Mix 1 ounce of strychnine sulphate with 1 ounce of baking soda and stir this into the hot starch paste to make a smooth creamy mixture free from lumps. Then stir in $\frac{1}{4}$ pint of heavy corn syrup and 1 tablespoonful of glycerine or liquid petrolatum. When thoroughly mixed pour this over 8 quarts of rolled feed Oats or Wheat and stir so as to coat each grain thoroughly.

If the bait is placed in runways it should be covered with a handful of straw or rubbish to hide it from birds. If no runways can be found place the bait in tiles or in long narrow cans near the base of several trees. The container should be placed so that no water will enter and it should be covered with straw to attract the mice.

Don't gamble on mice, they have their cycles and though you may get by for a year or two they are bound to turn up eventually and can ruin a young orchard in a single Winter.

Rabbits

Don't gamble on rabbits either. If they are present in the neighborhood of your garden you can depend on them to cripple or destroy every dwarf Apple tree. They will invariably attack your Apple trees first. But in the absence of Apples they will do an equally thorough job on any of the other fruit trees.

Because your dwarfs occupy such a small area a permanent rabbit-proof fence is much the most satisfactory solution. Apart from the problem of rabbits there are many advantages in fencing your garden of dwarfs. (See Fences.) But if permanent fences do not fit into your landscaping scheme a temporary fence of chicken wire tacked onto light stakes is, in my opinion, quicker, cheaper and surer than either of the other two methods. It need only remain in position during the three or four Winter months when forage is scarce or covered with snow.

Painting every branch and twig within likely reach of a Jack with a repellent paint is the usual remedy. Such paint is messy to prepare, useless unless prepared with care, rather expensive if purchased ready-mixed, and a nuisance to apply. If the branches are not absolutely dry when applied it may peel off leaving your trees defenceless and since the rabbits always work at night you may not realize what has happened until your trees are ruined.

The second method consists of various ways of wrapping or fencing individual trees. This is a simple matter for the first year or two when your trees are staked and with only a few pliable laterals but as they grow larger this method soon becomes very cumbersome.

How high should a wire fence be to stop rabbits? The only light I can give you on this point is based on my own experience. My trees are surrounded by a chain-link fence and over a long period of years the drifts frequently came perilously close to the top. When there was as little as 18 inches or less above the snow at several points I found numerous rabbit tracks up to the fence but whether or not they suspected a trap they have never yet jumped over those last few inches of fence. Fence companies recommend 4-foot fences as rabbit guards but I suspect that, apart from the problem of snowdrifts, a much lower fence would be equally effective.

Repellent Paint.

12 pounds lump resin (finely broken)

1 gallon cheap alcohol (anti-freeze type)

Be sure the alcohol contains no glycerine or other material which will affect its solvent properties. Tell the dealer and avoid disappointing results. Use lump resin not powdered resin. The latter contains a substance which prevents complete solution in alcohol. Crush the resin by placing in a sack and beat with a mallet or roll with a piece of heavy iron pipe. Sift through a fly screen to remove uncrushed lumps. Place alcohol in a large container and stir in the resin, very slowly, until it is all dissolved. This should make 2 gallons. The container in which the solution is to be stored should be dry and clean and should, when filled, be tightly closed to prevent evaporation of the alcohol. Keep the solution away from fire because it is quite inflammable. Pour a small amount into a small container such as a tin can for immediate use.

Chapter 5

PRUNING AND TRAINING

A WRITER for the *New York Times* introduced an editorial on Indian Summer by declaring that one could start an argument at any time in any company by simply attempting to define that term. In horticultural circles the subject of pruning is an equally sure-fire source of debate. In many cases each of two or more conflicting theories may be correct under the environmental conditions of climate and soil where they have been found to succeed.

In order to prune any fruit tree efficiently one must have some knowledge of its normal tendencies. We must know, for instance, whether its branches are naturally slender, open and spreading, or if it is weak-growing with early-ripening wood sparsely furnished with leaves or whether they are the opposite; whether it has a tendency to come into bearing early or late; whether it is a "tip-bearing" variety or bears its fruit on short spurs. With this fore-knowledge of what a given tree should look like at its successive stages, the art of pruning becomes a sort of juggling act, the balancing of wood-producing factors against fruit-bud-producing factors. One counteracts the other in normal trees and you cannot stimulate wood growth except at the expense of fruit-bud production. This is not to say, however, that you cannot simultaneously increase the production of wood growth and superior fruit. A weak tree might have abundant bloom but not sufficient foliage to ensure the satisfactory setting and maturing of large, perfect fruit. Let us begin, then, by stating the first principles of pruning. And at the top of that list we will place the dominant principle with respect to which nearly all others under the heading are direct corollaries or amplifications.

1. Anything that encourages wood growth will delay the production of and reduce the number of fruit buds.

2. Dormant pruning, nitrogenous fertilizers, optimum moisture conditions consistent with the health of the tree, intensive cultivation, and the use of invigorating rootstocks encourage wood production.

3. Summer pruning, root-pruning, relative dryness of soil, the practices known as "bark-ringing," "bending" and "twisting," and the use of dwarfing rootstocks check wood growth and promote fruit-bud production.*

4. Sap tends to concentrate at the highest point and thus we find that the highest bud on a branch grows the most vigorously and is the first to burst while those near the base are smaller and less likely to break into growth. But any bud can be made the highest by pruning back to it; the remaining buds increase in size and tend to develop either as branches or fruit buds.

   Apropos of the "highest point" see the discussion of "bending," "twisting" and "tip depressing" in the discussion of "Training."

5. The clean removal of a branch at its base has less effect either by way of checking by Summer pruning or stimulating growth by dormant pruning than if a stub with a number of buds had been left.

6. Dormant pruning of leaders has a more invigorating effect than the dormant pruning of laterals.

---

*Ample sunshine is necessary for the development of fruit. Nothing will take its place. Fruit trees, especially shy-bearing Pear varieties, may remain permanently unfruitful if planted in a too shady location.

Having stated the First or Fundamental Principles governing the reaction of growth to pruning we may now consider how these principles are applied in practice. And since this is largely a work of reference we have endeavored wherever feasible to present our information in the form of compact summaries. These summaries, as you will shortly observe, include information already dealt with elsewhere in this book but, as for instance in the summary "How to Hasten Fruit Bearing" where we borrow information from the chapters on Manuring, Rootstocks, Pruning and Training, we presume the reader would prefer a brief restatement to being put to the trouble of checking a series of references.

WHY WE PRUNE

1. To build a framework of the desired form and size.
2. To stimulate the production of wood when necessary, that is, to increase vigor.
3. To stimulate the production of fruit buds when necessary. (See spurring and root-pruning, pages 45-47.)
4. To remove a proportion of fruit buds already formed with the object of
    (a) preventing biennial bearing,
    (b) improving fruit,
    (c) conserving the strength of the tree—thus, in exceptional cases,
    (d) aiding in the setting of the remaining fruit buds.
5. To admit air and light, thus
    (a) facilitating dusting and picking,
    (b) improving fruit,
    (c) discouraging disease and certain insects.
6. To induce the formation of fruit buds close to heavy wood, that is, the operation known as "spurring," with the object of
    (a) improving fruit; the best fruit is borne close to heavy wood;

A.   B.   C.

FIG. 4.   PRUNING TO A BUD

A—Wrong. This cut will never heal over but will die back to bud and bud too may die.

B—Right. When the bud breaks into growth the shoot will quickly overgrow this short heel.

C—Wrong. Cut too close to bud which may dry out and die. Even if bud survives and forms a shoot it will break off more easily than if a slight heel were left.

(b) preventing w i n d - falls,

7. To stiffen the tree by producing f e w e r b u t stouter branches (the o p e r a t i o n known as "leader tipping," with purpose of

    (a) avoiding windfalls,

    (b) c a r r y i n g heavy c r o p s w i t h o u t breaking,

    (c) avoiding breaking due to sinking snow-drifts in Spring.

HOW WE PRUNE

1. Leader Tipping (for Apples and Pears). Leaders are those branches which extend the framework of the tree either by extending a branch or forming a new one. The tipping of a leader consists of removing, *when dormant,* anywhere from one- to three-quarters of it, the invigorating effect on the leader being in direct proportion to the amount removed. This increased vigor expends itself in the production of an increased number of vigorous laterals but the ultimate length of the branch is not as great as if it had not been tipped. This is because the terminal shoot of the tipped leader though longer than it would have been if the leader had not been tipped does not thereby fully compensate in length for the part that has been pruned off. Thus leader tipping is never used to

lengthen a branch, only to invigorate it. But, you may ask, would not the Summer tipping of leaders dwarf by not only shortening but checking the tree in accordance with number three of the above First Principles? That is certainly logical and partly true but in practice Summer tipping would tend to force into growth not only the terminal or uppermost but probably a number of others close to the top forming an unsightly plume-like cluster of parallel, vertical leaders and would have a harmful effect on the health of the tree. The desired effect (i.e., dwarfing a branch or shoot) is obtained instead by "bending," or "twisting," as described on page 49, "Repressive Practices," or cutting the leader back cleanly to a lateral which then becomes the leader.

2. Spurring (for Apples and Pears). Every branch on a tree is either a leader, a lateral, or a spur. If a lateral is allowed to increase in length and thereby extend or become part of the framework of the tree, it is said to be a leader. If it is in the process of being shortened to form a spur it is a lateral. When it has been shortened to about four inches (usually only a couple of inches) it is called a spur. Of course, it may be a natural spur and not require pruning. Thus every lateral eventually becomes a leader or a spur. As spurring is an essential and most important operation in caring for dwarfs it is dealt with separately and at some length later in this chapter.

3. Thinning. This consists of opening up the tree by cutting out (cleanly at its base) any leader or lateral for which there is not room without crowding. This work is ordinarily taken care of in the dormant season but a moderate amount of it may be done during Summer. In fact it is advisable in the event of a season of strong wood growth. Unless a tree is exceptionally open the fruit low down in the center is likely to be inferior and both spurs and laterals in

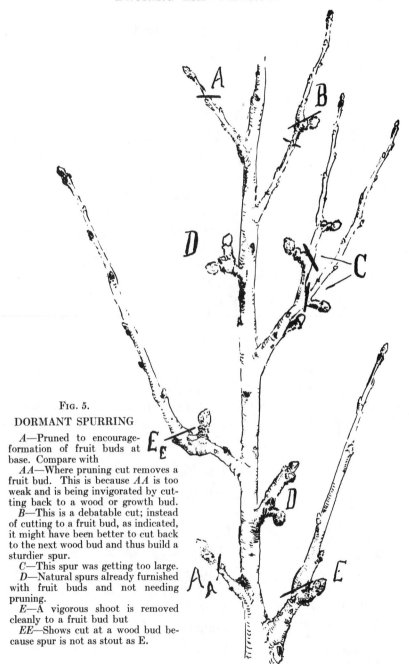

FIG. 5.

DORMANT SPURRING

A—Pruned to encourage-formation of fruit buds at base. Compare with

AA—Where pruning cut removes a fruit bud. This is because *AA* is too weak and is being invigorated by cutting back to a wood or growth bud.

B—This is a debatable cut; instead of cutting to a fruit bud, as indicated, it might have been better to cut back to the next wood bud and thus build a sturdier spur.

C—This spur was getting too large.

D—Natural spurs already furnished with fruit buds and not needing pruning.

E—A vigorous shoot is removed cleanly to a fruit bud but

EE—Shows cut at a wood bud because spur is not as stout as E.

that part should be removed at their bases.

PRUNING BUSH APPLES AND PEARS

1. THE YOUNG TREE

We have said earlier that one must prune to suit the individual tree. We must consider whether a tree is vigorous or slow growing, spreading or vertical, free-spurring or tip-bearing or whether it is an early bearing variety or not. Your nurseryman can tell you about vigor, bearing age and spur or tip-bearing. After the first pruning which is the same for all types and consists of severe leader tipping one can observe other idiosyncrasies of growth during the ensuing Summer season and prune accordingly. The function of each successive pruning might be described as follows:

(a) The First Pruning.

If it is a one-year-old, it may consist of a mere whip or it may have developed some laterals. Its pruning consists in cutting it back to the point where it is desired to form the head, about 10 inches or if a larger tree is intended, about 14 inches above the ground. This is done in early Spring if Fall planted, or at

FIG. 6.

HEADING APPLES

Head-quick to bear-Apples at 10 to 12 inches.

Head-slow to bear-Apples like Northern Spy, at 16 inches.

planting time if Spring planted. The
laterals, if any, are shortened to about
five buds but are not cut out: if it is
older then the first pruning should
consist of "tipping" (*i.e.*, shortening)
all leaders by one-third or as much as
one-half of their length.

The first pruning whether of one-
year-olds or older is invariably aimed
at inducing vigorous growth in addition to shaping the trees. By "vigorous growth" we mean a sturdy tree
with short, but well-spaced branches
and large, deep green, leathery leaves.
Some persons might suppose the term
equally applicable to the sappy, wil-
lowy, rank-growing tree with long,
smooth branches bearing few laterals
and no spurs, and with thin, pale foliage, the sort of growth associated with
too much shade and which is anath-
ema to the grower of dwarfs.

FIG. 7.

RESULT OF NO PRUNING

This two-year-old Yellow Transparent on Malling IX
is about 3 feet high. Instead of being headed at the usual
12 inches after its first year's growth it was left unpruned.
During its second growing season it added another foot
to its height and matured eight fruit buds, but produced
no framework. Failure to properly head a tree, as above
illustrated, is a mistake that is hard to redeem by subsequent care. It is better to start over again with a tree
that, as a result of correct heading, has wood buds properly placed for developing a low-headed sturdy tree.
Compare Fig. 8.

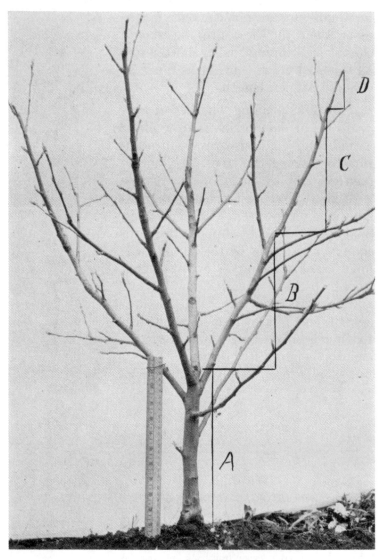

FIG. 8. RESPONSE TO PROPER PRUNING
(*Explanation on Facing Page*)

(b) The Second Pruning.

When we have had an opportunity to watch the reaction of the past season to the first pruning we can come to some conclusion as to whether the tree is weak and needs severe leader tipping or not. In any event, no matter how strong the growth is, the tree will require a certain amount of tipping if only to increase the number of branches. Normally one would remove perhaps one-half the leader or slightly less. If, however, the tree is at this time three or more years old a decision will have to be made as to whether immediate bearing with a consequent dwarfing effect is desired or whether a sturdier and usually rather larger, healthier tree is what is wanted. In either case, armed with a knowledge of the above First Principles, success or failure in pruning operations will now depend on how closely one observes the reaction of the trees—and an absorbingly interesting study it makes to watch one tree being forced into fruit bearing while an identical

RESPONSE TO PROPER PRUNING
(*Explanation of Facing Page*)

The photograph on the facing page illustrates response to proper pruning. The tree is an Astrachan Apple on Malling IX roots.

The successive four years growth are indicated by the letters "*A*" to "*D*". The base of "*A*" shows where the rootstock was originally budded.

A close examination will show that it has completed four growing seasons and has been dormant-pruned four times. As a one-year-old whip, or maiden, it was headed at 11 inches—see pruning scar indicated by extension of base line "*B*". During the ensuing growing season the four buds immediately below the pruning cut have made the most vigorous growth (the most vigorous growth is always just below the pruning cut as the sap flows most strongly to the highest buds). The next two lower buds produced two weaker branches.

The following points should be noted. (1) It is symmetrical; (2) The bearing wood is relatively heavy; (3) It is adequately furnished with fruit spurs; (4) The union between the rootstock and cion is safely above the soil; (5) It has just been pruned repressively (*e. g.*, the four strongest leaders have been pruned back to weak laterals).

This tree can be increased by several times its size or it can be retained at its present height of about 3 feet.

It matured three Apples in its third year—see fruit scars at extreme middle right.

neighbor with different treatment develops into an entirely different type of tree, even in one season.

2. THE ADOLESCENT TREE

Assuming that we have decided to bring the tree into bearing as soon as possible we now refer to the First Principles of Pruning. We have a deep-rooted dislike for rule-of-thumb instructions for the care of fruit trees; the reader must now use his own judgment. However, we can suggest the procedure for bringing a young tree into bearing, as follows:

(a) Cut back during the growing season all laterals intended as spurs (in accordance with the detailed instruction under the topic of "Spurring").

(b) Limit leader tipping to the removal of only a few inches, or omit entirely for one year.

(c) Thin as usual.

3. THE BEARING TREE

The routine pruning of the bearing tree is quite different with dwarfs than with standards. In the first place, the practice of spurring is never used in the case of standards since the trees are naturally less compact and there is less need for reducing laterals to spurs since they have sufficient space within the tree to be allowed to remain and carry fruit. Moreover spurring would be an economic impossibility owing to the size of the tree and the consequent difficulty of reaching the laterals high up in the tree. On the other hand, most dwarfs would soon be filled with a jungle of laterals if these were not thinned out or spurred. The spurring and thinning of laterals in vigorous dwarfs is an indispensible annual operation. The degree of tipping depends on the condition of each individual tree from year to year but some is always necessary.

PRUNING VARIES WITH DIFFERENT ROOTSTOCKS AND SOILS

It has been said that the world needs not so much to be told as to be reminded which prompts us to remind the reader that the above First Principles require us to balance the invigorating effects of a rich soil and vigorous-type rootstocks by tipping very lightly instead of severely (see Rootstocks).

Rule-of-thumb pruning of trees on weak and vigorous rootstocks might result in the normal bearing age of the trees on the vigorous stocks being advanced many years. On the other hand, lack of proper and regular leader tipping would normally result, in the case of weak trees, in too early bearing of heavy crops of small, inferior fruit.

SPURRING

Spurring is another much-debated question. Again it is no doubt true that the right method for Blackacres may be the wrong one for Greenacres, and so we fall back on our original recommendation namely, to apply the much-quoted First Principles and watch what happens.

You know what you want to happen. You want a thick short spur with at least one fruit bud. You want the fruit bud to produce fruit and sufficient leaves to nourish it. You want one or two growth buds to extend the spur another inch or so and culminate in a terminal fruit bud.

You likewise know what you want to avoid, you want to prevent the growth buds on the spur from developing into long rank shoots at the expense of the fruit now forming or of the fruit buds now developing for next year's fruit.

On the other hand, a moderate amount of wood growth in the spur is desirable to keep it healthy and productive. In the absence of sufficient wood growth the spur will tend to produce too much bloom, too little foliage, and to set too many fruits which must be thinned out and the fruits which mature will tend to be small. To remedy this condition the spur is cut back to a growth bud which, as a terminal bud, will grow more strongly than if it had developed below the terminal fruit bud. The shoot thus developed is then treated in the same way as any lateral intended as a spur. This treatment may be summed up as follows:

STEPS IN THE SPURRING OF A LATERAL

(1) About three or four weeks after shoot growth has started in the Spring, or when a lateral is 6 to 10 inches long shorten it by one-third or one-half.

(2) The end bud will probably break within a week or two and produce a new shoot extending the original lateral. To pinch this new or secondary growth too soon would check it too severely and it might even die. Instead, you allow it to grow on until it is 4 or 5 inches long when it is cut back (*i.e.*, the secondary growth) leaving only a couple of leaves. If it looks too soft and immature cut an inch or so back of the original cut.

(3) A few weeks later it may be necessary to repeat this operation but spurring should not be continued much past the early part of August since any subsequent growth might not be sufficiently ripe to withstand the Winter.

(4) The following Spring just before the buds begin to swell the spur should be shortened to five good buds.

The above four steps indicate how to spur where no fruit buds have yet formed. After fruit buds have started to form the advice is much simpler, you simply prune back to a fruit bud. This advice is qualified somewhat in the caption to Fig. 5.

It is better to err on the side of leaving a spur too long rather than too short. Some trees tend to produce fruit on long spurs and might be kept from bearing indefinitely. By leaving your spurs relatively long, you can observe the length at which a given variety tends to form fruit buds, whereupon you prune away any wood beyond such buds. It may also be accepted as a general rule that on young trees and vigorous laterals the portion left should be longer.

BARK RINGING

The actual steps in bark ringing are indicated in Fig. 9. Like root-pruning it should only be practiced where the less Spartan methods outlined under Pruning have failed to induce fruitfulness. But in the case of trees that are confirmed biennial bearers, or that refuse to come into bearing, or that are shy-bearing, it will prove an effective and practical remedy. It is particularly useful in the case of Pears; many varieties that have failed to bear or that have produced only token crops may be transformed into free-bearing trees even in one season.

ROOT PRUNING

The orthodox method of root pruning is to dig, in the Fall, a trench half way around the tree. It should be close enough to remove about one-third of the length or the roots encountered. A

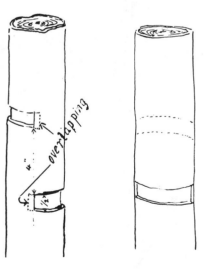

FIG. 9 BARK RINGING
Left—Side View   *Right*—Face View

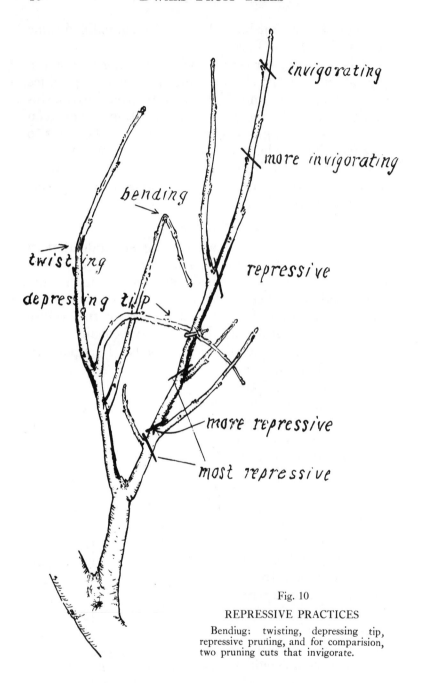

Fig. 10

REPRESSIVE PRACTICES

Bendiug: twisting, depressing tip, repressive pruning, and for comparision, two pruning cuts that invigorate.

year later the trench is extended to complete the circle.

Root pruning may be necessary with large trees. However, it is not difficult to dig up a dwarf and replant as above described. In this way you get to the real source of the trouble, the heavy downward-pointing roots. In root pruning you may, if you go deep enough, remove the extremities of such roots, but you have not changed their character. By lifting and replanting them horizontally and close to the surface, you have done something analagous to the bending or depressing of branches. In other words, you have checked the growth of such roots without imperiling the health of the tree. You have also promoted fruitfulness.

REPRESSIVE PRACTICES

Fig. 10 illustrates the following points: (1) Bending and twisting obstruct but do not stop the flow of sap to the tip. The buds immediately below the twist or bend are therefore not forced into growth as would be the case if the shoot had been pruned off at this point. (2) Depressing the tip of a branch arrests growth since sap flows most strongly to the highest point. In accordance with this rule the buds near the base, being now the highest, will break into growth. (3) Dormant pruning to a growth bud invigorates the branch so cut. (See leader tipping) (4) Pruning to a lateral is repressive and the weaker the lateral the more repressive.

FIG. 11. EXTREME RESULT OF REPRESSIVE PRACTICES

A further example of repressive pruning. It is an Astrachan on Malling II. Trees on Malling II are almost as vigorous as on ordinary standards and if left unpruned might grow 20 feet high. It has completed five growing seasons but has not yet fruited.

Chapter 6

EXTENDING THE PEACH BELT NORTHWARD

PEACHES, Nectarines, Sweet Cherries, Apricots, and the tender varieties of Plums and French Pears can be grown successfully many miles north of the so-called Peach Belt. This is accomplished by the proper selec-tion of rootstocks, by a careful choice of the kinds and varieties of fruit budded into them, and by taking some simple measures to protect them in Winter. We are able to point to a wide range of tender fruits grown in the open at Markdale, Ontario. Winter temperatures have remained well below zero for days at a time and extremes of 25 or 30 deg. below zero are not exceptional. According to a chart prepared by the local horticultural experiment station this garden is in the center of an area which is declared to be too cold for any except the hardier varieties of Apples. We believe this statement to be true in the case of standards. Markdale is 100 miles north of the so-called Peach Belt at an elevation of 1725 feet and 25 miles from the nearest body of water.

Damage to Wood. A clear understanding of the way in which Winter extremes of temperature damage or kill the wood of fruit trees will enable the gardener to more efficiently and intelligently apply the protective measures recommended in this chapter and elsewhere in this volume. The factors believed to increase resistance to Winter injury are:

(1) Ripeness.

(2) Vitality.

(3) Relative dryness (of branches—not of roots) coupled, however, with power to resist evaporation.

(4) Varietal hardiness, which includes such factors as dryness and early-ripening, the physiological implications of which are as yet largely unknown.

(5) Previous exposure to non-injurious low temperatures, which is possibly helpful in reducing excess moisture.

(6) Building up in the wood, by fertilizers or by mechanical introduction, substances which are believed to be helpful, possibly by increasing power to prevent evaporation. This is a line of investigation which will bear watching but which has produced no practical results as yet. See also Circular No. 156, New York Agricultural Experiment Station, Geneva, N. Y., for a discussion of diploids versus triploids.

Plant tissue is killed when crystallization of water within the cells ruptures the walls—or, by forming in the intercellular spaces, withdraws water from the protoplasm, thus destroying it. Cells vary greatly in their susceptibility to such damage so that not only different plants but different parts of the same plant show a wide range of resistance. It is important to know that, in addition to killing more or less cellular tissue, crystallization tends to dry out the part, whether branch or blossom and it has been well established in practice that if this drying out process can be artificially retarded many trees which would not otherwise survive may be saved. Brilliant sunshine is to be dreaded following a dangerous temperature drop since, even though accompanied by sub-zero weather, it raises the temperature of the bark of the tree to such a degree that rapid evaporation of free moisture take place. This process is speeded up by the presence of strong cold winds, which of course tend to become dryer as they become colder. It is principally with the object of offsetting these two drying agents, sun and wind, that fruit trees are wrapped with burlap since the temperature lag (so marked under wooden covers) is a comparatively negligible factor with burlap.

Damage to Blossom. For commercial growers winterkilling is a much less serious matter than damage to bloom by late Spring frosts. They simply do not attempt to grow trees that are not completely hardy in their district. On the other hand, damage to bloom is an annual hazard all the way from the Orange Belt to the most northerly limits of fruit growing. Consequently, any research that might result in ameliorating such damage would be of vast economic importance and, incidentally, very helpful in furthering the aims under consideration in the present chapter. Such research has been under way for many years in many countries and although nothing spectacular has yet been achieved it has resulted in a sounder application of existing remedial measures while some entirely new approaches to the problem have been discovered and are showing promise. An example of this is the attempt to produce resistance by the introduction into the plant of glycerine, sugar, and calcium chloride. Spraying with a dilute solution of glycerine decreased the susceptibility to frost damage on the same day and up to three days after spraying. However, until such period of resistance can be extended considerably, the method is not feasible. C. P. Field* suggests that—"If the fundamental reasons for resistance can be elucidated, they may point to remedial measures of practical value. Further, in the breeding of new varieties, attention to the characters which make for resistance in the selection of parents, may help to build up a race of varieties of commercial value which are at the same time less susceptible to the vagaries of the weather." On the results of repeated freezing and thawing he states that, "the low temperature must prevail for a certain minimum continuous period before damage results. This minimum

*C. P. Field Ann. Rep. East Malling Research Station, Kent, England 1941. "Low Temp. Injury to Fruit Blossom."

period is probably the time required for ice crystals to grow in the intercellular spaces in sufficient quantity to withdraw water from the protoplasm to a damaging extent. When this minimum period is not reached, it seems probable that the water can be drawn back by the protoplasm as thawing proceeds."

Winter and Spring Protection

To enumerate the different practices of Winter and Spring protection, we may

(1) Train trees against a solid wall of stone, brick, or wood.

(2) Lean wood covers against the walls.

(3) Mound the trees.

(4) Wrap bush specimens.

(5) Use windbreaks.

(6) Control moisture, fertility, and cultivation.

(7) Maintain vigor.

(8) Whitewash the trunks and main crotches.

1. Training Trees Against a Solid Wall.

Under "Training," instructions are given with a view to producing trained trees in relatively precise geometric forms with a view primarily to their decorative value. Such specimens involve attention and skill, whereas for the purposes of protection we need only to keep trees within certain bounds as to height and width. Also, they must be flat enough to permit leaning wood covers against them. Even with no knowledge of training anyone should be able to grow trees against a wall for Winter protection purposes that will produce satisfactory crops.

Solid stone, cement, or brick walls afford more protection than wooden ones and the face of a building is still warmer. South and west walls are, of course, the most desirable and any wall facing more than a very few points north or east of these two directions would be unsuitable. Morello Cherries are successful on east and north walls but because they are relatively hardy their training on walls is not necessary for their protection except in extremely cold districts. However, there is nothing more beautiful than a well-trained Morello Cherry in full bloom. Obviously the warmest walls are reserved for the most tender fruits. Whether a variety ripens early or late, training on a warm southern wall has the double virtue of extending the season during which the fruit will ripen properly and also speeding up that ripening process by a week or perhaps ten days, a total advantage of two to three weeks. There is a corresponding extension of the growing season in the Spring, the trees starting their growth at least a week earlier than the bush trees in the open. This is not desirable, however, since it increases the danger from late Spring frosts. (See Par. 11 under "Spring Frosts and Their Effects" for definite recommendations.) Pears and Apples do not succeed when trained against solid walls in most parts of America. The reflected heat is harmful to the foliage and the roots tend to dry out too much.

2. Lean Wood Covers Against Walls.

The garden is much in the background and deep in snow for the greater part of the Winter, so there is no need to use good lumber for the covers. Any old boards fastened together with a couple of battens would be quite satisfactory. The covers should be narrow and light enough for convenient handling. A few cracks will not matter but draughts are harmful. The covers should not be placed in position until the leaves have fallen and Winter weather has arrived. At Markdale this is usually around the latter part of November. In the Spring the covers are used to retard activity and should be adjusted in such a way that they will continue to shield the trees from the warm sun without trapping the warmth that will be absorbed by the covers. By reflecting instead of absorbing sunlight whitewashing trees prevents the alternate freezing and thawing of the bark during Winter and also prevents premature activity in the Spring. It would seem that whitewashing the covers might add to their effectiveness in retarding Spring growth and improve their appearance if, like our own, they are particularly disreputable. It would also help to preserve them.

3. MOUND THE TREES.

Most gardeners will agree that even where the Winters are mild a certain amount of Winter mulching will help any garden plant. This is particularly true of all dwarf trees because the roots of a dwarf are shallower than those of a standard. It follows, therefore, that in view of the trifling amount of work required dwarfs should always receive some Winter mulch. The most convenient material is earth but it should not be procured too near the tree. Manure is very efficient for this purpose but, as all gardeners are aware, it should not be allowed to touch the bark. Strawy manure should not be placed around the tree until quite late when the ground is frozen and the field mice have made their nests for the Winter. For the same reason, straw is inadvisable even though applied very late. Sawdust and shavings should never be used since, unlike the other mulch materials, they are not suitable for digging into the soil and, even though removed, a good deal would inevitably get spread around.

The amount of mulch required will naturally depend on how tender the roots may be and how severe the Winters; 8 to 10 inches deep at the trunk should be sufficient for the most tender roots and the hardier ones will be all the better for the extra protection. There is no comprehensive, comparative table of rootstock hardiness, but according to that rather mysterious, undocumented, unverified grapevine source of information known as "reputation" the Quince roots on which Pears are dwarfed are said to be somewhat tender. We might point out by way of reminder that the Peaches are usually dwarfed when grown on Plum roots which are relatively hardy. See Rootstocks.

The amount of snowfall must be considered when deciding what depth to mound since the depth varies widely depending not only on local climatic conditions but also on whether the snow piles up or is swept away by the wind.

4. WRAP BUSH SPECIMENS.

It is not necessary to wrap trees if they are under wooden covers. If they are the usual bush specimens growing in the open, very tender varieties should be wrapped. At Markdale we wrap bush Peaches, Nectarines, and Japanese Plums. We also wrap any tree which for any reason has been severely checked during the past Summer by reason of transplanting, injury due to insects or disease, spray injury, too-heavy cropping, or any other ordeal or mishap. Then again, we are guided by the condition of the wood, whether or not it has ripened well. It is normal in the Northern States and Canada for the Summers to be hot and dry and for the Autumn months to be cool and wet. But some Summers are so hot and dry that there is very little wood growth. If such a Summer is followed by an excessively wet Autumn Nature tries to make up for lost time by an abnormally lush and late Autumn wood growth which necessarily goes into the Winter in a very unripe condition. When this happens, we wrap twice as many trees as usual. By controlling the cultural factors (see No. 6) we can counteract the effect of such extremes.

The Sweet Cherry, though much hardier than the Peach, is supposed to be too tender for the Markdale climate but we have found that if the trees are kept small, planted where they will be sheltered from the prevailing cold Winter winds, and encouraged to ripen their wood well, they survive very low temperatures without wrapping. As a matter of fact, it is not possible to wrap the specimens grown in our orchard owing to the peculiar weeping form in which they have been trained. There is no sufficiently dwarfing rootstock for Sweet Cherries, therefore we are obliged to check growth by depressing all leaders. The trees eventually acquire a permanent umbrella-like form which would be impossible to wrap in the usual conical form.

As a first step in wrapping, decide whether the branches can be drawn together to form a single, conical bundle. This is usually possible with the younger and smaller trees but as they grow older, and the branches become more rigid, it is often more convenient to draw a number of lighter branches gently together towards a central and heavier branch forming two, or perhaps three, bundles. This sounds like an awkward and troublesome job but you must remember that the average tree is not more than 6 to 7 feet high and many of them not more than two-third that tall. It is really surprising how quickly one learns to speed up this operation so that it eventually becomes a matter of not more than two or three minutes. I save my burlap from year to year for this use. Selecting a length to suit the tree, secure a corner of the burlap to the base of the trunk and wind it in a spiral to the top where it is tied. One or perhaps two other ties of light cord will help to make the wrapping more airtight.

It is not too well understood why these wrappings are as effective as they are known to be. A tree that would be unharmed at a given low temperature might be killed by a temperature several degrees higher if accompanied by strong winds. It is also a familiar belief that many trees sustain Winter injury from the alternate freezing and thawing of the bark due to cold Winter nights followed by brilliant sunny days. (See Spring Frosts, page 64.) The relative importance of these two forms of injury has not yet been made the subject of any methodical inquiry since the wrapping of fruit trees has no commercial significance. The difference in temperature beneath the wrapping is so slight as to have a negligible effect. There is however a marked difference in temperature inside and outside the wooden covers. The protection afforded by the wood covers, in addition to shading from the sun, is due to the "lag" in the temperature fluctuations under the covers. For instance, the readings at sundown under and outside the covers might be 20 and 15 deg. above zero, respectively. The next morning you might find that your minimum thermometers registered zero and 10 deg. below, indicating a lag of 10 deg. If, on the other hand, the outside temperature had been 25 deg. below, the inside temperature might be 7 deg. below, indicating a lag of 18 deg. But if such an extreme lasted for a couple of days the margin may be reduced to 10 deg. Sometimes a strong south wind will suddenly send the outside temperature soaring to, say 35 deg. in which case the lag will be in the opposite direction and the under-cover temperature might perhaps be 28 deg. From these figures, typical of the results of several years' records, it will be noticed that before the trees under wood covers would be in danger of injury the outside temperature would not only have to be record-breaking but would have to persist without let-up for two or three days.

5. USE WINDBREAKS.

Anything that will break the force of the Winter winds is helpful but it is possible for a windbreak to do more harm than good under some circumstances. A

few years ago we set out a row of Lombardy Poplars in
the lee of a brick barn with a mansard or two-pitch roof.
For two years they grew absolutely evenly but after that
we had an increasingly graphic demonstration of what
a prevailing wind can do, for the trees next the barn
gained practically no height whereas, in a perfectly
symmetrical curve, those farther out were higher. The
ultimate picture suggested that someone had trimmed
the trees in a sort of scallop to conform to the downward sweep of the roof—only it happened instead to
conform to the downward sweep of the wind sucked
down by the roof. The point is that an obstruction that
merely deflects the wind so that it strikes the trees from
a different angle is not much help. It is ideal to have
a windbreak of evergreens which robs the wind of its
force but which is not sufficiently dense to act as a
pocket into which the coldest air will drain. This is a
special menace during blossom time.

6. Control Moisture, Fertility and Cultivation.

The control of cultural factors with a view to Winter
protection should be directed towards producing a normal Midsummer growth followed by as little Fall
growth as is consistent with the health of the trees. It
follows, therefore, that during an excessively hot, dry
period in Midsummer which tends to slow down growth
unduly you should practice intensive cultivation and
irrigation. Supplement this by a mulch of peatmoss,
strawy manure, or any other material that will cool the
ground and conserve the moisture. When a tree's
growth has been checked by drought and heat it is not
wise to attempt to stimulate it by the application of
strong fertilizers, although liberal applications of weak
manure water may be used to advantage especially if
subsequent attention is given to the maintenance of
moisture in the soil.

Cultivation should ordinarily cease by the middle of July and if the soil is becoming too dry this should be corrected by the use of mulch and irrigation, but never by cultivation. If the Summer growth is too rank there is only one remedy and that is the planting of cover crops. There is a wide choice and many opinions in this matter so that we may deal with the question in general terms by saying that any quick-growing crop that draws largely on the nitrogen in the soil would be satisfactory. Winter Vetch, Rape, Turnips, Buckwheat, Barley, and Rye are the crops often suggested. Buckwheat will make a very quick growth but will kill out with the first Fall frost, whereas Vetch and Rye, though slower to get under way, will grow late in the Fall and form a thick mulch which, in case mounding has not been attended to, will to some extent perform its functions. It prevents soil erosion, protects against extreme soil temperatures, delays alternate freezing and thawing, and can be dug into the soil as green manure in the Spring.

Following the disastrous temperature lows of 1933 to 1934, the New York State Agricultural Experiment Station published an interesting report indicating clearly the relationship between fertilizers and Winter injury,* from which the following is quoted:

*Circular No. 156

WINTER INJURY BY H. B. TUKEY AND K. D. BRASE

In one Baldwin orchard around 40 years of age, which had been used by this Station for fertilizer experiments for the past five years some specific relations between fertilizer treatment and Winter injury were apparent in the Spring and Summer of 1934. The fact that the orchard is particularly uniform as to trees and soil, and especially that the soil is acid and low in li·ne and has received 17 different fertilizer treatments, presented an unusual opportunity for studying the above relations.

As measured by apparent injury to limbs and branches after the trees had leaved out, individual trees showed injury ranging from 0 up to 80 per cent. The average for the orchard was 22.4 per cent. The general appearance of the trees improved as the season advanced so that by the middle of June the apparent injury was estimated as 12.7 per cent for the entire orchard. About this percentage of limbs or perhaps somewhat more was finally removed from the orchards.

There was a definite tendency for trees which bore a heavy crop in 1933 to show a greater Winter injury. It was possible to measure this factor because 23 per cent of the trees had their "off" year in 1933. This relation, however, varied widely with the various fertilizer treatments. Some of the treatments which gave the highest yields in 1933 showed a small percentage of Winter injury. In other words, although the tendency was for extensive Winter injury to accompany high yields of the preceding season, some of the fertilizer treatments overcame this tendency completely or in part. It is also significant that trees that were uniformly high yielders for the preceding four years showed the least injury. This means that trees that were well nourished by the proper fertilizer applications for this soil not only responded in yield of fruit but also best resisted the cold Winter of 1933-34.

As to individual treatments, it was found that on this acid soil, the surface of which at least is low in lime, nitrogen in nitrate form showed much less injury than nitrogen in ammonia form. When such ammonia-nitrogen carriers were supplemented with an application of lime or when they carried lime or other basic elements as constituents, the percentage of Winter injury was reduced. Alternate year fertilizer applications and in two cases Fall applications were not as effective as early Spring-applied fertilizers in fortifying the trees against the unusual cold Winter. These results show that to have a well-nourished orchard in which the trees have resistance to unusual environmental conditions such as low temperatures, specific soil and fertilizer characteristics must be carefully considered.

7. MAINTAIN VIGOR.

To state that the greater a tree's vitality, the greater is its power to survive Winter extremes would be axiomatic to say the least. And yet one might make the mistake of thinking that a tree which had made relatively little growth and had apparently ripened its wood thoroughly would be in an ideal condition to resist the Winter trials. But well-ripened wood is not the whole story, because the conditions which accounted for the small growth might also have sapped its vitality. There are many circumstances under which this situation might arise but by far the most frequent, and one against which we must constantly be on guard, is the mistake of over-cropping. Here you have apparently perfectly ripened but undernourished wood accompanied by a condition of lowered vitality which it may take a couple of years to correct. By judicious fruit thinning you not only increase the size of the fruit and prevent biennial bearing, but greatly reduce the danger of winterkilling. Again, in deciding on the relative Winter resistance of young and old trees our axiomatic rule is useful for it might be argued that the wood on a young tree being normally more tender and vigorous would be more susceptible to Winter injury than the older and better-ripened wood of a mature tree. But we find that, in spite of this, the younger and more vital tree is definitely more resistant to cold.

Insects, disease, incorrect pruning, transplanting, wrong fertilization, the overcropping we have just mentioned, spray injury, and, of course, Winter injury itself —all these lower vitality. Having sounded our warning that a devitalized tree requires extra Winter protection, what measures are required? The extra precautions recommended consists of higher mounding, extra thicknesses of burlap, and the wrapping of the vulnerable trees.

8. WHITEWASH THE TRUNKS.

In the Autumn the top of the tree is the first wood to ripen. Thus bark splitting and killing as a result of frost we note occurs in the trunk and the lower crotches at the base of the main branches. Whitewashing these parts of the tree has the effect of reflecting the sun and retarding the harmful warming and thawing of the bark following nights of severe frost. Whitewashing has been practiced with satisfactory results for many years in districts where extremes of night frosts and bright warm sunshine regularly alternate.

SPRING FROSTS AND THEIR EFFECTS

1. *Effect of Freezing on Flower Parts.*

(a) *Styles and Ovaries.* In the sequence of injury the loosening of the ovary skin comes first. This injury may only be temporary and flowers with no other injury may develop fruit. All the subsequent degrees of injury are probably fatal to the production of fruit. After this injury comes browning of the styles and petals, and later the browning of certain tissues within the ovary, the brown discoloration spreading from the styles, through the placenta to the ovules. By slicing a fruit bud with a razor blade the parts can be readily identified and the extent of damage determined by reference to Fig. 12. There are several practical advantages to be gained by such an examination. In the first place, it will provide an approximate indication of the relative resistance of the bloom of the different fruits or varieties. In making such a comparison, care should be taken to select blossoms at the same stage of development since there is some difference.

Unless the foliage needs dusting, you can dispense with dusting any tree on which no bloom has survived. Then there is the question of protective coverings. In the case of wall-grown specimens or very small trees over which some protective covering is customarily placed on the approach of dangerous frosts you may have the melancholy satisfaction of knowing that your ability to recognize lethal injury has saved you this trouble.

(*b*) *Anthers and Pollen.* The last parts of the flowers to be injured are the anthers and the pollen; they appear orange in color when killed. They are merely mentioned on account of the further clue they provide as to relative resistance.

2. *Temperatures Causing Damage.* Records of what constitute lethal temperatures for the different fruits are so conflicting that there is little to be gained by including comparative tables. For instance, three or four degrees of frost is usually considered quite cold enough to kill Peach blossoms and yet we were recently amazed to find that Peach bloom in our own garden

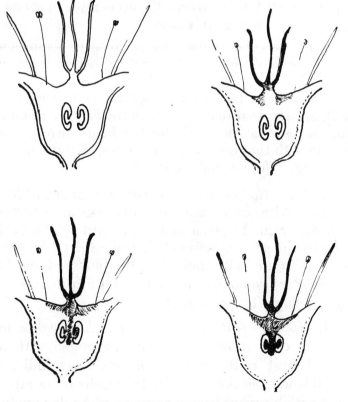

Fig. 12 SEQUENCE OF FROST INJURY TO FLOWER PARTS

within 10 feet of an accurate minimum thermometer which registered 20 deg. F. matured from 10 to 20 per cent of a normal crop. It might be said that thermometers are not infallible or that the duration of the drop was phenomenally brief but further corroboration of this surprising resistance was provided by the severe freezing of a nearby sumac in a more favorable position on higher ground and also by the blackening of the younger growth on a Virginia-creeper and a Black Walnut a couple of rods away, both of which were likewise on higher ground. Frankly, we would have been inclined to have mental reservations if anyone had asked us to believe that Peach bloom would withstand such a frost and so we can hardly complain if few Peach growers are willing to accept the accuracy of our observations or records in this case.

When we come to consider the relative significance of the degree of frost and its duration there is a gratifying uniformity in the results. We find that in an experiment with three different varieties the results were identical, namely, that in each subject the damage resulting from exposure at 29 deg. F. for two hours corresponded exactly with that resulting from 28 deg. F. for one hour or 26 deg. F. for one-half hour.

3. *Susceptibility to Cold at Different Stages of Blossoming.* With some exceptions the resistance to cold increases from the green bud stage until petal-fall. In one experiment it was found that at 28 deg. the green bud was injured after one hour, the pink bud and full flower after two hours, while the flower at petal-fall was injured only after three hours.

4. *Moisture Content of Flowers.* Although a low moisture content has often been associated with increased frost resistance, experiments have indicated that this was not borne out by the results of an experiment with blossoms from a selection of Apple varieties.

5. *Effect of Moisture.* Humidity of the air and soil moisture appear to have a negligible effect, but wet flowers are much more susceptible to frost damage than dry ones.

6. *Alternate Freezing and Thawing.* One of the most frequently emphasized, but inaccurate, statements in garden literature is that the alternate freezing and thawing of plants during the temperature extremes of the freezing nights and sunny days of early Spring is worse than continued freezing. This principle has been preached for too many years to be abandoned until it has been clearly disproven. In the case of Apple blossom, the series of experiments (Field 1941) already quoted above have demonstrated that "a single exposure to a low temperature for three hours proved much more damaging than several short periods adding up to the same time in the laboratory freezing chambers, but with intervals to allow them to thaw." There is still no doubt that the alternate freezing and thawing of the soil in which plant roots are growing is definitely more harmful than continuous frost but this may be due to the drying effect on the soil and it may be that if the moisture factor were kept constant it would be found that the roots, in common with the bloom, would suffer less from alternate freezing and thawing than from continuous exposure to the minimum low of such alternate temperatures.

7. *Rate of Cooling and Thawing.* Here again our fond beliefs have had to give way to the inexorable evidence of scientific experiments. We have always heard our elders say, and have firmly believed that in any plant the rate of freezing is immaterial but that rapid thawing must be prevented at all cost. It appears that, in the case of the Apple blossoms used for the experiment, the exact opposite was proven: "The slowly cooled flowers had only skin loosening, but in the rapidly cooled ones the damage extended to the ovules.

Thus the severity of the frost damage may depend not only on the minimum temperature reached but also *on the rate of fall of temperature.* Experiments on the rate of thawing were also carried out but *the damage was the same whether the blossoms were thawed rapidly or slowly."*

8. *Hardening of the Blossom.* When a severe frost is preceded by a series of mild non-injurious frosts the damage tends to be less than that caused by a sudden drop in temperature after a warm period. This was found to be true in the same series of experiments and, for a change, conforms to orthodox horticultural belief.

9. *Effect of Damaged Foliage.* Damage to foliage, by high winds for example, lowers the resistance of blossom to frost damage.

10. *Spraying with Cold Water.* In this series of experiments the spraying of blossoms with cold water after freezing had no effect.

11. *Retarding by Sprays, Shading, and North Walls.* Retarding bloom by hormone sprays is, for the present, little more than an interesting possibility. Retarding by Spring mulching of the frozen ground, by temporary shading in the Spring, or by growing trees on northern slopes, in relatively shady places, or trained against north walls are measures which have long been advocated by fruit growers as a means of retarding blooming. Unfortunately permanent shade would not only retard the bloom but would impair the health of any fruit tree. While some fruit trees are more tolerant of shade than others, every fruit tree mentioned in this book will produce better fruit when grown in full sunlight. Permanent shade, then, is a last resort and a doubtful solution at best. Planting on a northerly slope is a much better, alternative but the ideal way is to train tender varieties of Peaches, Nectarines and Apricots on walls where the tree can be kept in a dormant

condition longer by adjusting the wooden covers so as to provide shade without trapping warmth. Later on when in bloom the same covers can be used in an emergency. On account of their lightness cloth frames or curtains are preferable at this time and will provide a surprising amount of protection. It will be a most exceptional frost that will do serious damage to bloom under cloth covers. Of course, under wooden covers bloom is completely safe from any frosts that might come at that late season. Although discussed elsewhere we might mention the fact that Morello Cherries are universally recommended as being very tolerant of being grown on north walls or in partial shade although, as we have said, the Morellos in common with all other fruit trees would prefer an open sunny location.

Chapter 7

DWARF APPLES

THE DWARF Apple is the most eloquent argument in favor of dwarfs generally. In every way its advantages over the standard Apple are more marked than in the case of the other fruits. Dwarf trees fruit when younger. Better Apples can be grown on a pigmy of 3 or 4 feet than on a standard of 20 to 30 feet. In most districts Apples require more careful protection from disease and insects and trees of this size are easily dusted. And every variety of Apple may be successfully dwarfed.

Culture. In a discussion of the culture of dwarf Apples a few points need special emphasis. Apples are grown on the rootstock known as Malling IX, the only dwarfing stock that has thus far proven entirely satisfactory for home gardens.

If you have the selecting of your nursery trees, which you rarely do, you should choose a short, stocky tree with sturdy laterals low down on the trunk rather than at the top. Such a tree has grown vigorously and been severely pruned in the nursery. As a result of such treatment it should have no fruit buds. But whether you are fortunate enough to receive such a tree or have the bad luck to draw the long, slender kind, the cultural needs of either are thenceforth the same: Intensive cultivation followed by heavy mulching—barnyard manure if you have it, otherwise use half-decayed compost or one of the many other mulches. The mulch should be applied about the end of June and allowed to remain until Spring when it is incorporated with the soil. It will help if you draw it aside occasionally and cultivate the soil beneath. No cultivation should be necessary after the middle of August.

The roots of the dwarf Apple are so close to the surface, if it has been properly planted, that the mulch is a "must." It hardly needs to be said that great care should be taken to avoid injuring these shallow roots. The use of a mulch encourages a fibrous root growth that in some seasons can actually be seen at the surface of the soil near the trunk when the mulch is drawn back. When cultivating during the Spring and early Summer it is impossible to avoid destroying such shallow fibrous roots and under such circumstances cultivation must be more and more shallow the closer you get to the trunk. Care should be taken not to cut any of the permanent roots.

Malling IX or Jaune de Metz "Stock." This is the rootstock having the most dwarfing effect on Apples. And it is the only Apple rootstock that concerns us. Let us consider the natural tendencies of a quick-bearing variety of Apple tree growing on Malling IX. If given no pruning, merely routine cultivation and no mulching, it would probably bear its first fruit in its third year. It would be much more slender and weakly than the same variety on any other roots. In the succeeding years if the fruit were not thinned it would exhaust itself through overbearing, wood growth would come almost to a standstill, and with its diminishing vigor it would become a prey to pests and diseases of all kinds, its fruit would lack size and quality, and if it did not die it would at least become quite worthless at an early age. A depressing picture, no doubt, but one that can be prevented. A healthy, long-lived, prolific tree bearing fruit superior to standard Apple trees depends on several factors:

Prune hard for vigor when young.

Give intensive cultivation followed by mulching and feeding.

Prune judiciously after it comes into bearing.

Thin the surplus fruit when it tends to overbear.

Dust against disease and insect pests.

Compare Fig. 7 and Fig. 8.

How long will it continue to produce satisfactory crops? Let us be safe and say 20 years. But we have seen healthy Apples on this stock 30 years old and have heard of some healthy specimens of some 60 odd years.

Early Maturity of Fruit. Most dwarf varieties mature their fruits from ten days to two weeks earlier than when grown as standards. It thus becomes possible, by the use of this rootstock, to grow late-maturing varieties in districts where the Summers would otherwise be too short. Early maturity is characteristic of all kinds of fruit grown as dwarfs and is an attractive feature since their most important function is to provide a succession of fruits that can be used as they ripen. The period during which you can enjoy them is lengthened by that much.

Pruning. See chapter "Pruning and Training."

Training. There are several ornamental forms in which Apples may be trained but only three for utility 1. The ordinary bush which is vase-shaped and somewhat open in the center. 2. The pyramid, a specialized bush, in which the branches radiate from a central leader forming a broad-based cylinder. 3. The single cordon, a single stem furnished with short 4 to 5-inch spurs. (See Fig. 14.)

For the amateur the first and third forms are preferable.

In the ornamental forms the horizontal-trained tree (Fig. 15) is easily trained and quite striking.

In Fig. 16 are shown the measurements in the construction of a fence for horizontal trained Apples. It also shows a wavy wire known as "spring wire." It is worth an effort to get it at your hardware store. Its importance lies in its resilience. With Winter tempera-

FIG. 13 A YELLOW TRANSPARENT IN ITS FOURTH YEAR

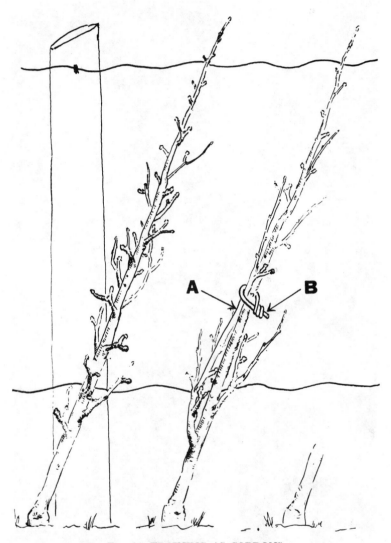

Fig. 14. TRAINING AS CORDONS

Apples or Pears Trained as Cordons on Wire Fence
A—Branch tied in to cover spurless section of main trunk
B—Willow wand used for tying

Fig. 15. HORIZONTAL TRAINED APPLES

Horizontal-trained Astrachan Apple on Malling IX

There are no hard and fast rules about spacing the tiers but 10 inches to 12 inches apart is usually satisfactory, the lowest being 12 inches to 14 inches above the ground. When young, precautions should be taken to prevent snow breaking off the lowest tier; that is what happened to this tree.

Compare the uppermost two horizontal branches to the right of the trunk with the corresponding two to the left. The vigorous growth of the former is the result of allowing the tips to grow upward. The meager growth of the latter is due to the growing tips being kept tied horizontally.

tures it contracts and straightens out but does not stretch. Snowdrifts drag it down but it springs back. And it remains taut for years. Straight wire, no matter how heavy, will stretch leaving branches unsupported and you will have the annual nuisance of tightening it.

The routine steps in developing a horizontal-trained tree are indicated by the figures but sometimes difficulties develop. The strength tends to flow into one branch at the expense of another. To correct this, you merely depress the tip or, if necessary, the whole branch of the too vigorous one while reversing the process in the case of the weak one.

The pruning of a cordon is identical (with one exception) with the spurring of a branch, the cordon being

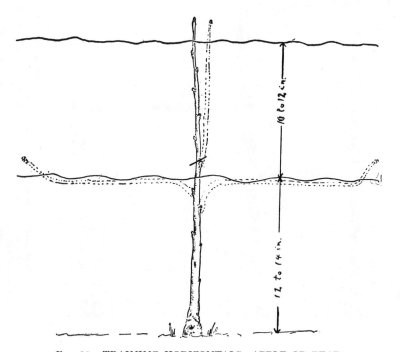

FIG. 16. TRAINING HORIZONTALS—APPLE OR PEAR

The first step in training a horizontal. Each successive tier is treated in the same way. The dotted lines show where the pruning cut has forced the three highest buds into growth.

simply a tree consisting of only one branch. The exception is that a cordon is never "tipped." If a cordon were a branch growing on a tree it would normally be shortened when dormant (see tipping of leaders) in order to invigorate and thicken it and help to develop a framework. A cordon has no framework to develop and, being supported by wires, and with possibly the further support of a bamboo cane, there is no need for it to develop a strong trunk. Furthermore leader tipping discourages the production of fruit spurs. And since our aim is to furnish our cordon evenly with fruit spurs from ground to tip the conclusion is obvious: never prune the leading shoots of a cordon. A bamboo cane in addition to keeping the cordon straight makes it very easy to slope it as it grows taller—it is vertical when young but is eventually sloped at an angle of 45 deg. Note where well spurred branch has been tied in to cover a spurless section of main branch.

By far the best tie for training is the willow wand (Goat Willow—*Salix caprea*). If space permits you should grow a clump. You merely shove the base of a dormant willow wand into the soil in Spring and then forget about it. If all else fails that Summer you will be sure of at least one flourishing plant. If you do not choose to grow your own you will find them growing in any nearby swamp. Or your nurseryman will let you have some of the supply he keeps on hand for tying bundles of nursery stock.

Cross-Pollination. The reader no doubt remembers from his school days the story of how a flower is fertilized. He will recall that the flowers of some plants have male or staminate blossoms only, whereas others bear only female or pistillate flowers. The pollen from the stamens of one plant must reach the pistil of another in order that the ovules at its base may be fertilized and develop into seeds and cause fruit to set. There is a third type of flower, the perfect flower, in which both stamens and pistil are present. All fruit tree blossoms belong to this third class and should in theory be independent of outside sources of pollen. There are many exceptions and the Apple, as a class, is one of them. In other words, the pollen of every Apple variety is, in varying degrees, incompatible with its own pistil. Therefore, every Apple variety should be cross-pollinated by some different Apple variety.

In most home gardens there are different varieties of Apples or your neighbor has some, in which case there will likely be adequate cross-pollination. It is therefore hardly necessary to discuss this matter in detail. If you are only planting two or three Apple trees and they must depend on each other for pollination you should have your nurseryman advise you as to their ability to cross-pollinate.

Winds normally do not carry fruit pollen and the only reliable distributor is the honey bee. When that admirable insect starts to work on Apple blossoms he touches nothing else until the Apple nectar crop has been completely harvested. Any other insect dilly-dallies about from clover to Apple to buttercup with no order in his life and relatively little effect on the Apple crop.

Choosing Varieties. All varieties of Apples can be grown as dwarfs on Malling IX roots. Nurseries list fewer varieties as dwarfs than as standards. This situation will steadily improve and may eventually be reversed.

In choosing your Apple varieties you will have in mind diversification, hardiness, succession, dessert and culinary quality. If planting only a few, they should be Summer and Autumn varieties that you can enjoy as they ripen. One of the greatest advantages of growing your own dwarfs is that you can pick each individual fruit at the precise moment, and it is a brief one, when it has attained absolute perfection. If you have already taken care of your Summer and Autumn needs and have space for some Winter Apples you will discover an almost equal, though different, pleasure in carefully packing and storing them. There can be few moments in a man's life that offer more profound contentment and satisfaction than that afternoon in early Autumn when he sits before a hamper of McIntosh Reds filling a box with some choice specimens for a friend or wrapping some extra fancy ones and carefully packing them in the familiar, red-painted box marked "Christmas."

Hardiness need not be taken quite so seriously for dwarfs as for standards; nor for home gardens as compared with commercial orchards. The commercial grower of standards stakes his livelihood on his trees. He has to wait long years before they produce even a sample of fruit, then years more before they begin to produce profitably. To compensate him for the expense of these many years of care he wants an almost positive guarantee that they will continue to be profitable for at least another 30 or 40 years in spite of the worst Winters that may come along. The grower of a few dwarfs doesn't need to be that careful. Moreover his dwarfs survive with the help of a mulch and a blanket of snow and with the protection from Winter winds usually afforded by home buildings and fences. An orchard of standards may succumb when exposed to the drying effects of cold Winter winds which also sweep the ground bare of snow.

Nevertheless, while he can afford to gamble on hardiness he should take care to have one or two really hardy Summer Apples such as Yellow Transparent, or better still its descendant, the Lodi, which is larger and not subject to biennial bearing. The Red Astrachan is quite acid as a dessert Apple but unexcelled for cooking or jelly, and looks wonderful on the tree. For a Winter Apple which combines high quality with extra hardiness, nothing can compare with the familiar McIntosh.

There are some even hardier Russian Apples but their quality is far inferior. The Yellow Transparent and McIntosh have survived 40 degrees below zero in my garden with no perceptible injury to the wood and obviously no harm to the fruit buds for they bore average crops that Summer. However, there is no doubt that while a tree may survive a severe Winter it does not escape unscathed; it is weakened and less able to withstand subsequent ordeals.

It cannot be overemphasized that with regard to varieties you should seek the advice of successful fruit growers in your district. For example, every fruit has its own very exact preference as to soil and climate and you should try to find out which ones find your conditions most congenial. Nothing short of actual tests can provide the answers. In this way you can eliminate some varieties from your list but there are bound to be many that have never been tried locally that are ideally suited for your garden. In view of what has been said, it is clear that no list can be perfect except for a given locality and in most localities only a limited number of varieties have been tested. The list that follows is therefore only tentative.

HIGH QUALITY APPLES FOR THE HOME

(Listed in order of ripening. d=dessert, c=culinary)

Yellow Transparent. See Lodi.

Lodi. d, c. A descendant of the Yellow Transparent, it is better than its parent. The fruit is larger, ripens a little later and the tree bears annually. It is quick bearing and very hardy.

Astrachan. d, c. A hardy, showy Midsummer red. Acid but excellent for applesauce or jelly.

Melba. d, c. It is mildly and pleasantly flavored and highly aromatic. Apart from its other good qualities it is easily the most beautiful Apple in my garden. It is large and symmetrical and an unusual bright crimson. From my personal observation the fruit seems to be specially resistant to disease and insects, and seldom has a blemish. It is rather quick bearing and hardy.

Early McIntosh. d, c. This variety ripens about a week later than Lodi. It is hardy, productive, requires thinning early and severely to prevent biennial bearing. It is not as good quality as Melba nor nearly so attractive in appearance.

Gravenstein. c. The fruit is striped with red. It is a most excellent Autumn cooking Apple. It lacks hardiness. The new Red Gravenstein has all its parent's excellent qualities plus a much more attractive dark red color. It is rather quick bearing.

Milton. d, c. This is the McIntosh type but a month earlier, a beautiful pinkish red with heavy bloom. Being a cross between a Yellow Transparent and McIntosh it has the tendency of the former towards quick bearing and of the latter towards annual bearing, also the hardiness of both parents. It should be chosen in preference to Wealthy.

Fameuse (Snow). d, c. It is a high quality Apple that diversifies your collection by its snowy flesh and distinctive flavor. But it is very susceptible to scab which disfigures and dwarfs the fruit. As a dwarf tree it makes a poor cordon and is rather difficult to manage in bush form. It is disappointingly slow to come into bearing. I have never observed it as a dwarf except in my own garden and it may make a more satisfactory dwarf under different conditions.

McIntosh. d, c. This is the hardiest Apple in this list with the possible exception of some of the new McIntosh-type Apples which may equal it. It has every virtue and deserves its great popularity. It comes into bearing fairly early, bears heavily and annually, and is very productive. It is at the top of my list for its season.

Sweet McIntosh. d, c. It is a new Apple and, although I have no acquaintance with it, the New York State Fruit Testing Cooperative Association of Geneva, N. Y., has this to say of it—"It suggests McIntosh in appearance, flavor and aroma. The variety is, of course, primarily adapted for home use—for baking and to eat out of hand. It should become a splendid home and roadside market sort. Dr. U. P. Hedrick describes it as "the best sweet Apple" although that honor is awarded by the Association to the Sweet Delicious.

Grimes Golden. d. Its beautiful golden color lends contrast and interest to a collection of trees. It has a tender, crisp flesh of good dessert quality.

Macoun. This is another of the McIntosh type but darker red and even better flavored. It is slower to come into bearing and tends to overbear and to be biennial.

Delicious and its Red Sports. Since 1895 when this variety was introduced its popularity has risen until there are now planted in the United States more trees of Delicious than of any other Apple variety. Well grown it is at the top of the list, but an undersized Delicious is worthless. If it does well in local orchards you should by all means include it. In districts where it fails as a standard it may nevertheless succeed as a dwarf. It requires heavy feeding. In cool districts it should be grown only as a cordon or horizontal-trained specimen since it will get more sun and attain greater size than when grown as a bush.

Sweet Delicious. d. This is exactly what its name implies, a Delicious plus extra sweetness and very high quality.

Northern Spy. d, c. See Sandow.

Sandow. d, c. This is a very high quality Apple, better than its parent, the Northen Spy. It is also hardier and comes into bearing earlier.

Winesap. A good flavored bright red Apple for the South. An excellent keeper.

Golden Delicious. An excellent, richly flavored yellow, if well grown.

PICKING APPLES

A rough rule for any fruit is that it is ready for picking if, when tipped up and pulled gently, it parts easily from the branch. Some Apples should be picked several days before this stage is reached if they are intended for cooking; for example, Yellow Transparents intended for green Apple-pie.

Chapter 8

DWARF PEARS

THE Pear is the fruit *par excellence* for the amateur. The difference in quality between the Pears he can grow in his own garden and those he can buy in the market is probably greater than in the case of any other kind of fruit. There are a number of reasons why this is so but by far the most important is that he can pick it at exactly the right time and give it the exact period of after-ripening it requires. Picking and after-ripening is a fine art but one easily acquired by a discriminating lover of fruit.

It is also true that dwarfing improves the quality and increases the size of Pears more than of the other fruits. For example, Duchess as a standard is rather granular and lacking in quality but dwarfed on Quince the texture is good, the flavor is excellent, the size is increased, the crop is more dependable and, in fact, there is such an all-round improvement that commercial orchards almost always grow this variety as a dwarf.

Culture. In contrast to these glowing tributes the remainder of this chapter contains some rather sobering considerations. The first is that the soil must be right. Pears are dwarfed by budding on Quince roots. For best results these demand a rather heavy clay loam. Such a soil usually provides the even moisture without which dwarf Pears will not be satisfactory. Any gardener who attempts to grow them on light, loose soil will need to be very resourceful in the use of moisture-conserving mulches and constantly on the alert against drying out.

The remarks on mulching contained in the preceding chapter on Apples can be applied to Pears. But it is not quite so imperative since Quince roots are not so close to the surface and, if desired, cultivation can take the place of mulching.

Again, may I remind the reader to consult local fruit growers about his problems. He can refer them to a neighbor or the nearest commercial orchardist. Or he can write his nursery or the nearest state experiment station. Soil is one such problem. Is it heavy enough for Pears?

If he is told that Pears will not succeed under his local conditions it may be that there is still an interesting choice of other fruits which do thrive and he will concentrate on these. If, on the other hand, he has his heart set on Pears the chances are he will find a few varieties that are tolerant of his conditions. In too light soil he can dig in humus and clay; if he lives in a district where fire-blight is severe he will experiment with blight-resistant varieties such as Seckel, Bosc and (if he must have Pears regardless of quality) even the despised Kieffer—the most resistant Pear of all.

Climate. In the matter of climate the conditions for success are again exacting. It must not be excessively hot or cold and there must not be sharp fluctuations. The required conditions prevail in many sections of Europe but America for the most part has anything but an equable climate both temperature and moisture conditions being subject to violent extremes. Perhaps that is why, unlike its more tolerant relative, the Apple, America has no native Pear.

What to do about the climate? Obviously, one cannot do much in commercial orchards but it is possible to do a good deal about it in a home garden of really small dwarfs. To moderate the effects of extreme Midsummer heat temporary portable shading will prove effective and it is not too cumbersome for 5 or 6-foot trees. Then, of course, there are the hot climate varieties, Kieffer, Le Conte and Garber, which are too low in quality to find a place in gardens where any other varieties will succeed but have the redeeming features that they will tolerate the climate of the Gulf States and are highly blight-resistant.

Under home garden conditions Pears can be grown much farther north than is possible in commercial orchards. In a garden they usually have the important advantage of more protection from cold Winter winds; the snow accumulates and protects the roots; a mound of soil a few inches deep can be thrown against the base of the tree just before the solid freeze-up and a mulch of strawy manure on top of this will guard the roots against any temperature the tops can survive. Do not forget that mulching should be applied as late as possible to prevent mice establishing their nests in the mulch. Remember also that mounded soil shrinks and exposes a tender ring of bark if applied too early. Under comparable conditions many of our high quality Pears are as hardy as the Northern Spy Apple.

If Pears are well protected from winds and are mounded and mulched as above there should be no injury from a few brief dips down to 20 or even a very quick dive to 30 deg. below zero. Provided, of course, that they are healthy and vigorous specimens, that cultivation has been suspended early enough to allow them to ripen their wood, and that they have not been weakened by overbearing or by attacks of insects and disease.

It is impossible to be dogmatic in discussing killing Winter temperatures. Far too many factors are involved. It may, however, be helpful to state the climatic conditions under which my trees are grown and what injury and losses have been sustained. In the past 13 years there have been two dips to 40 deg. below zero. The first was deadly but the second only killed the odd tree. All of them as a result of the latter Winter suffered more or less from "black heart," a dark discoloration of the wood, but have grown and cropped well during the three seasons since that ordeal.

It would be very misleading to suggest that Pears generally will survive—40 deg. or even—30 deg. Where such temperatures are recorded special precautions should be taken. Only the hardier varieties such as Flemish Beauty should be grown in bush form and these should be planted where they will be sheltered from the prevailing Winter winds. For this reason they should be kept rather small. The less hardy varieties should

FIG. 17. PEAR BUSH

The pyramid form in which this Pear is trained is well adapted for Pear varieties of a vertical habit. In this form it occupies very little space.

Courtesy of Gardens and Gardening, The Studio Publications, Inc., New York be trained as horizontal or fans and in these forms it is a task of only a few minutes to tack a protective cover of burlap around the fence on which they are trained. The fence should be made with slats or wire but should not be solid. Pears thrive on solid walls in the moist, moderate climate of England or parts of Europe. In this country the reflected Summer heat of a wall is likely to be harmful to either Pears or Apples. Of course a solid wall plus Midsummer shading would be ideal if any one were prepared to take that much trouble.

Pruning. See chapter "Pruning and Training."

Training. The advice about training Apples is, for the most part, equally applicable to Pears but there are a few distinctions. Unlike the Apple, many Pear varieties lend themselves to training as pyramids, that is to say, as broad-based cylinders. This is because of their vertical habit of growth. But there are others, Beurre Superfin, for example, which have slender, spreading branches and these though impossible as pyramids make ideal horizontals.

Fig. 18.   HORIZONTAL PEAR CORDON

Sometimes trained this way along borders. A method favored in France but except for its saving of space or its novelty value it is not to be recommended. It interferes with cultivation and is easily damaged by subsiding snowdrifts. Vertical cordons are much to be preferred.

Courtesy of Gardens and Gardening, The Studio Publications, Inc., New York

Some European texts have lists of Pears especially recommended for growing as cordons. These are varieties which form fruit spurs very readily. But any Pear can be grown as a cordon by simply tying in against the main trunk sufficient branches to provide the necessary number of fruit spurs. (See Fig. 14.) The same method may be followed in the case of Apples such as Northern Spy which spur very poorly on the lower part of the main cordon trunk.

Pears Are Dwarfed on Quince Rootstocks. The Quince has been used in Europe for centuries to dwarf Pears and in America for well over a century, whereas the Malling IX Apple rootstock is relatively new. Unlike the Malling IX dwarf Apples in America, the dwarf Pear has always had a place in commercial Pear growing. There are commercial orchards of Malling IX dwarf Apples in England catering to the tray fruit trade—the uniform fancy quality Apples so'd from trays in the city streets—but it is very doubtful if they would be commercially feasible under present conditions in America.

The danger of cion-rooting has been emphasized. (See Page 19.) If the union between the Pear cion and its Quince rootstock is covered by soil the Pear will throw out its own roots sooner or later—in most cases. But there is much less danger than in the case of Apples. By removing some soil it is comparatively easy to ascertain whether this has taken place and to prune away the offending Pear roots if it has.

Certain soil conditions are less favorable than others for cion-rooting and in such cases the union should be covered for there are a number of very good reasons for doing so. Where winter killing is a problem there will be less danger if it is covered 1 to 2 inches deep and the risk of injury from the Quince borer will be eliminated. There will also be less risk of breakage at the union. If, however, the union is more than 2 to 3 inches above the

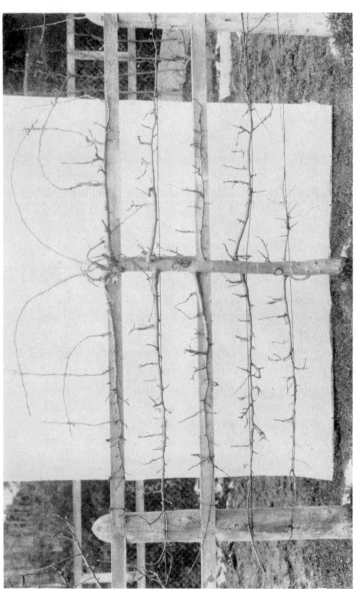

FIG. 19.   HORIZONTAL-TRAINED BEURRE SUPERFINE PEAR

When the lowest branch was broken off by snow a shoot was bent around from the opposite side and has now replaced it.
Note how several vigorous branches at the top of the trunk have been bent down rather than pruned off.
Some Pear varieties tend so strongly toward vertical growth that it would be almost impossible to train them as horizontals.
When ordering, you should mention your intention of training it in this form and ask your Nurseryman to substitute a Pear of
similar season and quality but one with a more spreading or pliable branch formation in case your selection is too rigid and vertical.

roots it may not be possible to cover it without planting too deeply.

Compatibility of the Pear Cion with Quince Roots. There are three types of Quince rootstocks, A, B, and C. Pears grown on C are weaker growing and earlier bearing than the other two although all three are about equally vigorous for the first few years. The three types for all practical purposes are identical in the matter of compatibility or incompatibility with Pear varieties. Quince C is a fairly recent introduction and may not be generally available for some time. Quince A (also called Angers) is the one most generally used and is ordinarily satisfactory. A Pear on Quince C will require less pruning, will come into bearing earlier, and will be relatively more productive. This is especially true under some conditions of growth, also in the case of varieties that grow strongly on Quince, and for some forms of training such as the single cordon. Quince C has not been under observation long enough to quote actual data on its effect on shy-bearing varieties but there is little doubt it would make them more productive.

All fruit from Pears with Quince roots is better colored, better flavored, often better textured, and always, in varying degrees, larger. This is true notwithstanding the fact that the variety may be highly incompatible with its Quince roots; provided, of course, that the incompatibility does not interfere with the normal development of the foliage.

Incompatibility may appear in different forms: the tree may be unthrifty from the beginning; it may start off well and then become moribund; it may flourish and crop perfectly for a few years and then, almost overnight in midseason, it may wilt and die; or it may break off at the union. It is apparent, therefore, that it is not a conclusive proof of compatibility to point to a healthy appearing, heavy cropping tree; there must be some assurance that it will continue to crop well for a sufficient number of years to make it worth while.

The following varieties are universally acknowledged to be entirely compatible with Quince and to have outstanding advantages over the same varieties on Pear roots: Duchesse d'Angouleme, Beurre Hardy (the variety most often used in England for double-working), Louise Bonne de Jersey, Flemish Beauty, Beurre Diel and Easter Beurre.

The following are all satisfactory on Quince and some of them are, no doubt, fully as compatible as some in the preceding list but not so generally recognized as being so: Conference, Anjou, Beurre Clairgeau, Beurre Superfin, Laxton's Superb, Doyenne Boussock, Buffum, Dana Hovey, Clapp's Favorite, Tyson, White Doyenne, Elizabeth, Howell, Lawrence, Jargonnelle and Josephine de Malines.

The following are incompatible in varying degrees, some failing to grow when budded into Quince whereas others will have every virtue, being vigorous, healthy, quick to bear, but having also the fatal defect of deteriorating at the union and eventually either breaking at that point or suddenly dying. Bartlett is an example. They should be double-worked, that is, a completely compatible variety such as Beurre Hardy should be budded into Quince and the incompatible variety budded into the Beurre Hardy, the latter thus bridging the incompatibility. Here belong: Bartlett, Bosc, Marie Louise, Seckel, Winter Nelis, Dix, Columbia, Paradise, Dunmore, Sheldon and Washington.

Pollination and Fruit Setting. Few, if any, Pear varieties are completely self-sterile but all benefit greatly by cross-pollination. A very few, for example, Seckel and Bartlett, are inter-sterile. Others do not cross-pollinate because their blooming periods do not overlap.

Inadequate pollination may be the cause of failure to set or of subsequent dropping of the newly set fruit but both these troubles may also be traced to other causes. The weather may be responsible. Rain may wash away the pollen; winds, rain and cold, alone or combined, may prevent the flight of bees; and if it is too cold the time required for the pollen to grow down the pistil may be unduly prolonged with the result that the pollen disintegrates and loses its vitality.

You can do a lot to minimize the effect of these conditions. You should see that at least two varieties are planted, almost any two will do (excepting Kieffer, which produces poor pollen, and excepting Seckel and Bartlett which are inter-sterile) provided they bloom at the same time. If you have enough fruit trees to make it worth while you might persuade a neighboring apiarist to place a hive of bees in some out-of-the-way corner, for your mutual benefit. A very important aid is to see that your Pear trees are in a sheltered position and yet exposed to full sunlight. If in a bush form they should be kept free of unfruitful sucker growth and if necessary a few of the branches can be bent down because this slows down wood growth and induces the formation of large, well ripened, well nourished fruit buds.

In my garden a number of Pears were grown in pots until five years old. They received the same fertilizer treatment as the check trees in the open ground. None of them fruited. They were then removed from the pots and planted in the open ground. Five years later one of them made a half-hearted gesture but the half dozen fruit that set all dropped. At ten years of age not one had matured a single fruit.

Everyone might not agree with me on the lessons to be drawn from this experiment. However, these are my conclusions: Although the pots were sunk in the ground, the roots, being confined, did not provide sufficient nutrients to build up plump fruit buds and although they bloomed they failed to set. After they were planted in the open ground their continued failure to fruit was due to the initial check they had received; their roots had become adapted to nourishing only wood growth and an unchanging quantity of leaves. In other words, these trees had formed an unfruitful habit.

From the melancholy case of the potted Pears we can draw a lesson in reverse: During the first few years you should aim at a steady, uninterrupted, vigorous but not rampant growth; avoid checks due to drouth, weeds, insects and disease, or failure to cultivate. If your tree fails to set fruit on schedule bending down a number of branches so that their tips point downward will hasten fruiting on such branches and establish the fruiting habit.

Picking Pears. Nearly all amateurs leave Pears on the tree too long. A Pear is usually ready for picking when the green of the unripe fruit gives way to a shade that has none of the mellowness of ripeness but faintly forecasts it. At that time it is stone hard.

PEARS ADAPTED TO PARTICULAR NEEDS

Hardy Varieties. Flemish Beauty, Tyson, Seckel, Elizabeth, Lawrence, Beurre Giffard, Dana Hovey, Winter Nelis, Conference, Duchesse d'Angouleme, Anjou, Idaho, and Sudduth (the hardiest and poorest in quality).

Blight-Resistant Varieties. Kieffer, Garber, Le Conte, Sudduth—all very poor in quality; Seckel, Tyson, Duchesse d'Angouleme, Buffum, Doyenne, Boussock and Beurre Giffard, of good quality but not so resistant.

To provide a Succession from Midsummer to Winter. Beurre Giffard, Elizabeth, Laxton's Superb, Tyson, Clapp, Bartlett, Seckel, Conference, Bosc, Dana Hovey, Anjou, Duchesse d'Angouleme and Winter Nelis.

Chapter 9

DWARF PEACHES, NECTARINES, AND APRICOTS

IN A GARDEN which has known 40 deg. below zero twice in the past ten years it may surprise you to know that the fruit that gives me the greatest all-round pleasure and satisfaction is the Peach.

It is not merely a controversial or academic opinion but a thoroughly tested conclusion that Peaches are very desirable subjects for the home garden in any climate where the hardiest Apples will succeed. I simply train them as fans against walls that face in any of the 16 points of the compass from east to west with due south being best and, if cold enough to warrant it, with the added protection of wooden covers.

Culture. If Peaches can be obtained which have been budded on the Plum rootstock, Saint Julien C, you can grow them in any soil that will grow good vegetables. Being a Plum root, it is tolerant of moist, heavy soils. Of course, all fruit trees benefit by good drainage. Unfortunately, you may be able to obtain only Peach on Peach rootstocks and in that case you must see that drainage is perfect or else be prepared for failure. It used to be thought that Peaches could only be grown on light sandy or gravelly soils, but it now appears that the virtue of such soils was in their perfect aeration and drainage.

If your soil is heavy and lacks aeration there are a number of ways of adapting it for Peach roots; in other words, of lightening and opening it so that it will admit air. Sand immediately suggests itself but it is of rather doubtful benefit; a better way is by the addition of lime, manure, and compost. And, of course, it is understood that perfect drainage has been provided in the form of a layer of broken pots or crocks or other flat over-lapping material placed at the bottom of the planting trench. Undertiling may be desirable.

The foregoing refers to the preparation of the soil for planting. With the emphasis still on drainage, the soil should be deep, not less than a foot and a half. This may mean building up a broad shoulder in front of your fence to provide the extra depth of soil. Digging into the subsoil would not do unless the water which would collect in such an excavation could be tiled away, and even then it would be less satisfactory than building up a shoulder.

Cultivation around established trees which will aer-ate the soil should be as frequent as time permits. But by the end of August you can put your hoe away and broadcast some Fall Rye on the loose soil. The first rain will wash the seed in or you can water it yourself—in either case it germinates very readily. It will make rapid growth if there is sufficient rain and will perform its triple function of helping to ripen the wood, protect-ing the roots by mulching and holding snow, and adding humus when worked into the soil the following Spring. If potash is worked in around each bearing tree in Sum-mer it will protect it from disease and help to sweeten the fruit. If available, use a pail or two of unleached hardwood ashes. It contains 3 to 7 per cent potash, a trace of phosphoric acid and 30 to 35 per cent calcium or lime. Potash fertilizers, such as potassium sulphate or potassium chloride, may be used just after growth starts in the Spring, about half a pound to each bearing tree—keep it at least 18 inches away from the base of the tree.

In ordinary good garden soil the only other fertilizer that should be necessary is bonemeal which provides 23 to 25 per cent phosphoric acid. It is in an unavailable form; therefore the season of application is unimportant because its effects will extend from one year to another. If, however, the foliage lacks vigor and the rich green of good health, it may need nitrogen. This should be applied with caution in the form of sodium nitrate or in a balanced commercial fertilizer. It is better to use about a half of the amount prescribed by the manufacturer, repeating the application two or three weeks later if no improvement appears. Nitrogenous fertilizers should never be applied later than the middle of July.

Pollination. All the familiar varieties of Peaches are completely self-fruitful.

Pruning and Training. Peaches and Nectarines are identical in every way excepting for their fruits. On walls or fences they are always trained as fans. As fans they require altogether different treatment from the other fruit trees.

It is essential, or at least very desirable, to start with one-year-old whips (maidens). Prune back to a height of 1 foot when planting in the Spring. That Summer five shoots are tied into position. Those growing towards the front or back and any superfluous ones, are removed as soon as the five are chosen. As the Summer advances some of these shoots may develop more vigorously than the others and these are retarded by depressing. At the same time, tie the weaker shoots in a more nearly vertical position.

Before growth starts the following Spring these five shoots are shortened by one-half. That Summer each of the five branches will be allowed to develop two strong shoots making ten branches in all.

During the next dormant pruning, i.e., 24 months after planting, these ten branches are again shortened, this time by only one-quarter. The 20 branches that are produced that Summer form the permanent framework of the tree.

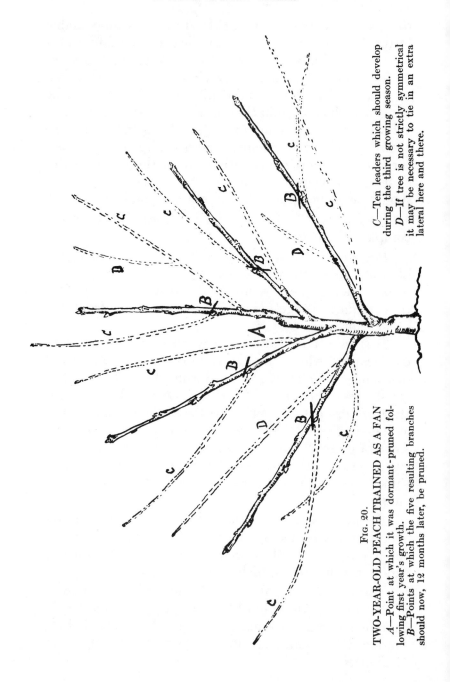

Fig. 20.

TWO-YEAR-OLD PEACH TRAINED AS A FAN

A—Point at which it was dormant-pruned following first year's growth.

B—Points at which the five resulting branches should now, 12 months later, be pruned.

C—Ten leaders which should develop during the third growing season.

D—If tree is not strictly symmetrical it may be necessary to tie in an extra lateral here and there.

Thenceforth the skill of the gardener will consist in encouraging strong new growth close to the base of the tree to replace the wood which, as it grows older, tends to produce its strongest laterals farther, and farther from the base. This will eventually require drastic pruning of old heavy wood back to shoots arising close to the base. If healthy, such a shoot need not be large because it is capable of astonishing growth even in one season if not crowded and if allowed to grow upright. See Fig. 20 for the above operations.

From the permanent framework lateral shoots will provide the fruit-bearing wood. Each such shoot should be managed as shown in Fig. 21 and as explained in the caption accompanying it.

Bearing shoots are spaced about a foot apart. When growth starts in the Spring these shoots are treated as shown in Fig. 21. Immediately after the fruit has been harvested, each shoot is cut back to the shoot that was allowed to develop at its base. Then the latter is tied in to replace it.

The disbudding as illustrated looks laborious. Actually you will find it so at first but you will soon improvise some method for speeding it up. Personally, I evolved a system that has become automatic. I grasp the upper part of the branch in my left hand and with a downward sweep of my right remove both fruit and shoots from the upper third. The remaining two-thirds I treat less recklessly because most of the fruit must be left until the final fruit-thinning stage. I knock some of the shoots off with a brush of my hand, the others I break off one by one.

It requires considerable vigilance to prevent the terminal shoot from robbing the branch of its strength. Actually its only purpose is to draw the sap and so it is only allowed to develop three to six leaves. Thenceforth, all new growth on it should be pinched out.

Insects and Disease. If your garden is north of the so-called Peach Belt you may be entirely free of both

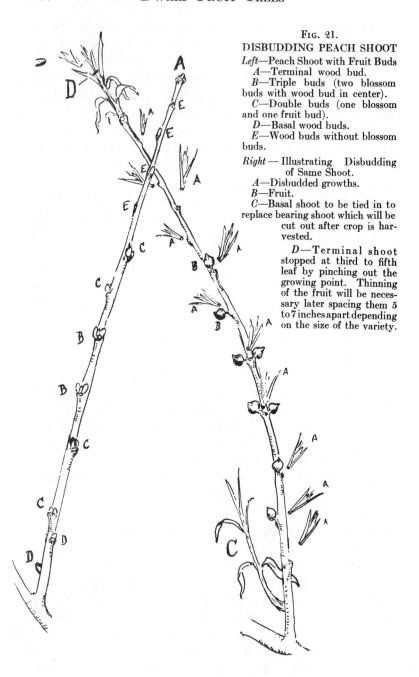

Fig. 21.

DISBUDDING PEACH SHOOT

Left—Peach Shoot with Fruit Buds
    A—Terminal wood bud.
    B—Triple buds (two blossom
buds with wood bud in center).
    C—Double buds (one blossom
and one fruit bud).
    D—Basal wood buds.
    E—Wood buds without blossom
buds.

Right — Illustrating   Disbudding
        of Same Shoot.
    A—Disbudded growths.
    B—Fruit.
    C—Basal shoot to be tied in to
replace bearing shoot which will be
        cut out after crop is har-
        vested.

    D—Terminal shoot
stopped at third to fifth
leaf by pinching out the
growing point. Thinning
of the fruit will be necessary later spacing them 5
to 7 inches apart depending
on the size of the variety.

disease and insects. If you are in Peach territory you will have the usual assortment of both. With small bush trees you should have little trouble in protecting them because they are more open to air and sunlight and also because of the ease with which you can dust them. Obviously, the same reasoning applies with even greater force to fan-trained Peaches.

There are two insects attacking Peaches which cannot be controlled by the all-purpose dust already discussed, the Peach borer and San Jose scale. In the home garden the Peach borer can be spotted by the exudations of gum and sawdust borings from its tunnels close to the ground. Unlike the Apple borer which penetrates deeply into the heartwood the Peach borer is found just underneath the bark and so can easily be located and destroyed. In commercial orchards paradichlorobenzene is spread in a circle a few inches away from the trunk. But in the home garden the mechanical methods are better; you can either work a wire up into the hole or cut away the bark above the channel until you locate the borer. Though the remedy is simple it must not be neglected as this insect can quickly kill a tree. If your trees are attacked by scale you may be obliged to apply an oil spray or the dormant lime-sulphur spray in accordance with your local spray chart, usually at a dilution of 1 to 9. The tree must be completely dormant at the time of application.

Harvesting.—Peaches, like Pears, require exceptionally careful picking in order to get the best flavor and texture. Some of the white-fleshed varieties are at their best when eaten dead ripe direct from the tree. The other varieties should be picked as soon as they develop a mellow color, at which time the flesh will give slightly between finger and thumb but will not dent.

The Nectarine

This is a desirable home garden fruit but even when fanned against walls fails to attain its full sweetness in cool Summers. In warm seasons it has a richer flavor than the Peach. Although the fruit does not resemble a Peach, the tree is identical. Not only are the tree characters the same but, being a sport of the Peach, a pit from a Nectarine may produce a tree bearing Peaches, or vice versa. It is even recorded that fruits of Peaches and Nectarines have developed simultaneously on the same tree.

Apart from the fine quality it develops when it is well grown, the Nectarine with its shiny rich red, or yellow and red skin is very beautiful when trained as a fan. It is self-fertile and cross-fertile with Peach varieties. It is well worth your while to try one at least. Surecrop, an Australian variety, is described by the New York State Fruit Testing Cooperative Association as "large, roundish, white and overlaid with a very attractive red. The flesh is firm, tender, free from the stone, and very pleasing in flavor; late midseason. If only one Nectarine can be grown Surecrop should be elected." Early Rivers and Stanwick Elrudge are two English varieties I have found satisfactory in my garden although they lack flavor in cool seasons, particularly the latter variety. They require jarring to get rid of the Plum curculio.

APRICOTS

The reason we hear so little about the Apricot is because it blooms ahead of any other fruit and as a result the bloom is frequently killed by Spring frosts. When trained against a wall it can be protected easily. If in Winter wooden covers are leaned against the wall these can be adjusted in the Spring in such a way that they will shade the trees and thus retard blooming. Even if a hard frost should come along after the covers have been stored away it will take only a few minutes to throw a cloth over the wall and anchor it with a board or a few stones.

The Apricot should be trained as a fan. Like the Peach, there will be a tendency for the branches to become bare near the base and for the vigor to be concentrated towards the ends of the branches. This must be corrected by pruning out such branches or by bending them down in such a way that the strength may be diverted into some young shoots nearer the base.

If you are unable to obtain Apricots on dwarfing rootstocks they are likely to be on Myrobalan rootstocks and if so the resulting tree will be quite vigorous. In that case you should rely on bending, that is to say, depressing the leaders or vigorous branches and doing as little pruning as possible. It may also be necessary to dig up the tree and, when replanting, flatten out near the surface any strong downward-pointing roots—the ones responsible for rampant wood growth. Root pruning is a drastic measure and, although sometimes necessary, the above method is safer and usually effective.

Apricots are self-fertile.

Chapter 10

DWARF PLUMS

MANY an amateur will find the Plum the most fascinating of all fruits to work with. If you had nothing but Plums in your garden, a representative collection would provide you with fruit of such diversity of color, form, size, aroma, flavor, and texture that you would hardly miss the others. Even the trees provide contrasts of form and coloring, the light green foliage of the Imperial Epineuse standing out against the darker shades of the other Europeans.

FOUR MAIN GROUPS

1. The Domestica or European group (*Prunus domestica*) contains all the highest quality Plums and where they will succeed you will have little interest in any varieties belonging to the other groups except perhaps one or two of the tart ones, like Shropshire Damson, that make the best jam. You would also want at least a couple of Japanese varieties even if only for the aesthetic thrill of their profuse bloom and the beauty of their ripe fruits.

2. Japanese Plums (*Prunus salicina*) are the least hardy group but some members of it, Burbank, Abundance, and First, are fully as hardy as most varieties of the Domestica group. They have the defect of blooming earlier than the Domesticas and crop failures due to late frosts are more frequent.

3. The species *Prunus insititia* gives us (a) the Saint Julien C discussed under the topic of Rootstocks,

(b) Mirabelles, small delicious dessert Plums, golden yellow or green, and (c) the Damsons, used only for jellies and jams for which purpose Shropshire is well known and the best. This group is hardier than the Domesticas and is rated by some as being about equally as hardy as Apples.

4. Native or Americana Plums comprise several species. They are important only in those regions where the Winters are too severe for the other groups. Hybrids between the native and the Japanese Plum have retained the hardiness of the one parent and much of the appearance and quality of the other, and so the true native Plum even in its own realm of the far north is relegated to a position of very little importance in home gardens and none at all in the commercial field.

Culture. If Plums are sold as dwarfs they may be on selected Americana roots or on Saint Julien C. If on either of these they will be tolerant of a wide range of soils but will do best on rich clay loams. If on the extremely dwarfing Bessey Cherry (*Prunus besseyi*) they will prefer a lighter sandy loam but will tolerate heavier soils provided they are well drained.

Plums on Saint Julien C are likely to be very hard to find since they are unpopular with nurserymen owing to the slowness with which this rootstock can be multiplied in the nursery. The Bessey Cherry is ordinarily used as a rootstock for the hardy Hansen hybrids and, for the present, few other varieties will be found on it. It is quite possible that your local nursery will be able to offer you nothing but Plums budded on Myrobalan, a relatively vigorous rootstock. But you need not postpone your adventures with Plums on that account. With the right management, you can get along very nicely with Myrobalan. You will have a little longer to wait for your first fruit, perhaps one or two years longer. You will have to take steps to check wood growth; in addition to routine pruning you will have such operations as depressing leaders, root pruning or transplanting.

Give careful attention to these matters during the years before it begins to fruit. Later, fruiting will absorb a lot of the surplus vigor and you should have no difficulty in maintaining it as a healthy, productive dwarf tree 6 to 8 feet high.

Checking Root Growth. It may be that some of the varieties on your list tend to be unusually vigorous under your local conditions of soil and climate. In that case, a further check may be necessary, you may have to plant your trees in a container that restricts the roots.

A 12-inch or 14-inch flower pot is the best container since a wooden box will decay within a couple of years, usually at the corners. However a box may be used, one made of heavier material but about the size of a butter box (14x14x14 inches).

The container is then sunk in the ground until the rim is barely below the surface, say an inch or less. The coarse, downward-pointing roots, the ones responsible for the unwanted vigor, lose themselves in the bottom of the container in a vain attempt to penetrate the drainage material and escape through the drainage hole —vain only if the greatest care is taken to block them by providing 2 or 3 inches of flat overlapping layers of broken pots or similar material (see Fig. 2). The smaller, more fibrous surface-feeding roots will quickly flow over the rim of the container and in the course of a year or two some will tend to become coarse and vigorous and this will soon be reflected in the increased vigor of the top. The remedy is not to cut out such roots but to lift them and replant them horizontally and close to the surface. Attention to this operation will not only reduce the vigor but greatly hasten the time when the tree will come into full bearing.

When planting in containers it will be necessary to crowd the roots into as small a bundle as possible without breaking them. The soil used should be fairly heavy, rich, and rather fibrous but not loose. Sod-pile soil is the best; it is usually composed of alternate layers

of inverted sods and cow manure. These are allowed
to decay and are then mixed. If you don't have this,
the next best will be the soil from your compost heap;
and lacking either you will have to get along with ordinary garden soil to which some coarse peat moss has
been added. To any of these types of soil there should
be added some charcoal and three or four handfuls of
bonemeal. The latter is very slow in its action and a
handful or two more than necessary will do no harm.

It should be dug up after two years to see that no
roots are getting away, excepting over the rim. If several trees are planted in boxes it will of course only be
necessary to lift one of them in order to check the roots,
a matter of only a few minutes. If pots are used and you
are quite sure the broken crocks are performing their
dual function of providing drainage and preventing the
roots reaching and plugging the drainage hole they may
remain permanently in the ground. But unless the
greatest care is taken it is frequently found that the
drainage hole has been solidly plugged with one large
root with disastrous effects on the roots remaining in
the now waterlogged pot.

A further advantage of using containers is that you
can conserve space by sinking them close together.
Later, as they become crowded, you can lift alternate
ones and move them to permanent locations.

Training. In the home orchard the question of
whether you train your tree as a pyramid or with a
vase-shaped or round head is of little importance. To begin with, the uniformity of tree size sought in commercial orchards is out of the question in the garden. Your
aim will be to have no duplication of varieties but rather
the maximum diversification. If you have a dozen Plum
trees you will find yourself using a dozen different methods of training. For instance, the Japanese varieties require totally different treatment from the Domesticas.
The Japanese varieties require severe pruning, both
before and after coming into bearing, and renew their

wood rapidly. In this respect they resemble the Peach,
whereas most varieties in the Domestica group should
be pruned as little as possible because, as a class, they
are slower to come into bearing.

The Domesticas, especially if on Myrobalan roots,
will send up very vigorous vertical shoots from 3 to 5
feet long and these should not be cut off; instead they
should be depressed and tied as shown in Fig. 10. The
reasons for depressing branches are: (1) to hasten
fruiting (2) to avoid stimulating the wood growth
which would result from removing such branches when
dormant (3) to avoid the shock to the tree which would
be caused by removing such large branches during the
growing season (4) to avoid the risk of infection getting
into the pruning wounds.

Though the practice of bending greatly reduces the
need for pruning, and a little judicious root pruning will
limit it still further, there will always be some thinning
to do. It is important that this be done annually so
that, relative to the size of the tree, the same amount
of wood is removed each year. Apart from these recommendations Plum should be trained and pruned in accordance with the principles of pruning set forth in
the chapter "Pruning and Training."

It is not too low to have the first branch of a dwarf
Plum 1 foot above the ground. By heading as low as
this the total height of the tree is less, there is less danger of breakage at the union or of uprooting, and injury
to the bark of the trunk, which sometimes results from
bright Winter sunshine, is minimized.

Plums are easily trained as fans but are not very
well suited for any of the other espalier forms. If they
are hardy enough to succeed as bushes with no protection that is the way you should grow them, reserving
for the tender fruits such as Peaches or Nectarines any
suitable walls or solid fences. Even where the latter
are perfectly hardy it is still preferable to use the walls
for training Peaches since they are rather more attract-

ive than Plum fans and the fruit benefits more from the extra sun.

Pollination. Some Domesticas are completely self-compatible, others are partially so, and still others are not at all self-compatible. But even a self-compatible variety probably benefits by cross-pollination particularly in the colder districts or in unfavorable seasons. Any two Domesticas will do provided their blooming dates coincide. Most Japanese Plums are self-incompatible and must be cross-pollinated by another Japanese although the Domestica, Reine Claude, will pollinate the Japanese Shiro. Any Japanese pollen is effective on any other Japanese variety with the sole exception of Burbank which will not do for Shiro although Shiro will pollinate Burbank.

Picking. Plums should likewise be allowed to completely ripen on the tree but, owing to their tempting rich color, they are frequently picked too soon and eaten before they are fully mellow.

Black-knot. This is mentioned only because so many gardeners have the erroneous idea that it is a serious menace. Actually in a garden that receives any spray or dust it will probably never appear but if it does it can easily be cleared up by cutting out and burning the affected branches.

Brown rot. Unheard of under some climatic conditions, brown rot must be carefully guarded against in other locations. In a few places, some parts of Japan for instance, it has been found impossible to control it in commercial orchards. If it is troublesome in your district your nurseryman will be able to recommend varieties which are resistant to it.

Plum Curculio. This insect needs watching for only a short period, just about a week to ten days in my garden. But that is all the time it needs to ruin every fruit on every Plum tree. An all-purpose dust contains a stomach poison which will control most of them but enough will survive to do some damage. You should therefore supplement your dusting with "jarring." The emergence of this insect varies in different environments. In my garden the first usually appear early in June or when the fruit is a little bigger than a bean. If you think they are about due you should not wait for them to begin operations. First you place a sheet under a tree in the comparative coolness of the early morning. Then you jar the tree with the heel of your hand or some kind of improvised rubber mallet. The colder the morning the more easily they can be dislodged. When you examine the sheet you will find what look like tiny, dry, gray lumps of soil. Even when held in your hand they may still fool you unless you examine them closely. If you find no insects the first time you might wait two or three days before trying again provided you see no sign of the familiar crescent cut on the young fruits.

When they do appear, you should jar the tree for a couple of successive mornings and then on alternate mornings for the rest of the week. By that time you should be able to discontinue jarring but for another week you should look each day for any new injury. In spite of your vigilance there will be a certain number of stings and since such fruits are worthless if the egg develops you should nick it out with the square corner of a razor blade. The crescents are easily spotted and if your tree is low and you can reach all the fruit from the ground it takes only a few minutes to run through the tree with your razor-blade knife and remedy the damage.

Varieties. Since you should in any event consult your nurseryman or state horticulture station when choosing varieties of Plums which will coincide with your preferences and at the same time succeed in your district, it has been thought unnecessary to suggest lists in this text. Rather different considerations have made it advisable in the case of Apples and Pears.

Chapter 11

DWARF CHERRIES

No FRUIT is without some drawback. Pears have blight, Apples have scab, Plums have curculios and Cherries have the birds. I have a friend whose house looks across the road at a commercial orchard of a couple of hundred Cherry trees. Spread over that many trees the loss per tree from birds could not, he reasoned, be more than a half-dozen or so Cherries. So he planted right along the road and directly opposite the Cherry orchard an assortment of three Cherry varieties. When they came into bearing the birds used to strip them clean before touching a single Cherry across the road. Whether or not in his indignant recounting of these circumstances a suggestion of hyperbole has crept in, it is certainly true that a gardener who plants one or two isolated unprotected Cherry trees does not stand a chance against the birds. He can, however, protect them by training them (1) as small bush trees with all branches tied down forming a weeping or umbrella-shaped tree or (2) by growing them as fan-trained espaliers along a fence (the better way of the two). In either of these forms they can be conveniently covered with a bird-proof netting. Or he can plant enough trees to satisfy the local population of robins and cherry-birds and still have some left for himself. In English gardens it is not uncommon to find a large wire enclosure within which all fruits requiring protection from birds are planted. This has always seemed to me a somewhat extreme measure and, even though built with considerable care, such a structure would detract greatly from the appearance of any garden.

If, having been warned, the reader is prepared to meet the challenge of the birds he will find that the Sour Cherry has practically no other black marks against it and almost every virtue. Less can be said in favor of the Sweet Cherry. Sour Cherries come into bearing younger than the Sweets but not so young as Peaches; in other words, probably in their fourth or fifth year from the bud, that is, in the second or third year in your garden if purchased as two-year-olds. They are about as hardy as the Northern Spy Apple, bear regularly and heavily, and are not hard to protect from insects and disease except in climates where brown rot is troublesome. Both the Sweet and Sour Cherries are ripe well ahead of any other tree fruits being weeks ahead of the first early Apples. The first Sour Cherry pie ushers in the culinary fruit season while the early Sweets, allowed to become dead ripe inside their bird-proof netting, will be a reminder of the difference in quality between those that are eaten fresh from the tree and those purchased in stores even though purchased within a day or two of picking.

Culture. The Sweet Cherry is perhaps a little less hardy than the average Domestica Plum, but the Windsor variety in otherwise congenial environment seems to be about equally as hardy. The Sweet Cherry purchased from most nurseries will be found to be on Mahaleb roots and though it will be slightly dwarfed as compared with one on Mazzard stocks it will tend to become too large for a garden of dwarfs unless the repressive measures indicated in the Plum chapter are drastically applied.

Of course, you may be fortunate enough to obtain both Sour and Sweet on suitable dwarfing stocks in which case you will have an earlier bearing and a more easily managed tree. The English Morello, even on vig-

orous Mahaleb and Mazzard, is a small, shrubby, quick-
bearing tree but it is still smaller on Sour Cherry Stocks
such as Kentish or Stockton Morello. The other Sour
Cherry trees are rather small even on vigorous rootstocks and you should have no difficulty holding them
at any desired size.

The difference in the cultural needs of Japanese and
Domestica Plums is somewhat analagous to the difference in the demands of Sweet and Sour Cherries. In
each case the first is more tender, prefers a lighter soil,
and is less tolerant of poor drainage although in this
respect the Japanese Plums would survive where the
Sweet Cherry would die. And both the Japanese Plums
and the Sweet Cherry resemble the Peach in their ability to quickly replace wood that has been pruned away
and, at the same time, to continue to develop fruit buds.

The Sweet Cherry is the biggest problem for the
grower of dwarfs. It is normally rather slow to come
into bearing, hard to hold down to dwarf dimensions
even on suitable rootstocks and in spite of repressive
measures and it is dangerous to prune owing to its susceptibility to disease and rots that enter the wounds.
If in addition to these objections the climate or soil or
drainage are not favorable, you might better confine
yourself to the sour varieties. But if you are prepared
to give them the rather special culture they demand,
there is no reason why they cannot be grown as dwarfs
in almost any garden.

Sour Cherries will succeed in a wide range of soils but
prefer a deep clay loam; the Sweets are much more
exacting and should have a sandy or gravelly soil that
must never become wet and at the same time must
never become too dry. Both benefit by regular cultivation.

Training. We have mentioned the need for training
Cherries in a weeping form or as fans on fences in order
to protect them from birds. The weeping or umbrella-

shaped tree is formed by tying the leading branches to weights placed on the ground. It will require two years before the wood will set rigidly in this position. In the meantime strong vertical shoots will develop from the buds at the highest point on the looped branches. Some of these can be similarly tied down either to lower branches or to the ground weights but others will have to be cut out cleanly at their bases.

The fan form is, however, preferable. Sour varieties as fans require a 6-foot fence but Sweet Cherries will be much more easily managed on a fence 8 or 9 feet high. A well-trained Cherry fan is one in which all main branches radiate from near the base and the horizontal branches close to the ground are as vigorous as the vertical central ones. Since the strength flows strongly into the vertical branches, at the expense of the horizontal ones, it is necessary to attain an approximate balance by temporarily reversing their positions by bending. If, however, the central branches have gained too great a lead, you may have to cut one or two of them out at their base near the ground and fill in the space by tying in laterals from adjoining leaders. The pruning of main branches, as above, should be done in the Spring before the buds break. But a moderate thinning of the current season's growth, especially the too-vigorous lateral shoots toward the ends of the branches, may be done throughout the season. These shoots must be cut away cleanly at the base.

Pollination. All Sweets require cross-pollination but all Sours are self-fruitful.

Picking. Cherries are picked when dead ripe.

Varieties. Of the two Sour strains, the Morellos and the Amarelles, by far the best of the former is English Morello and of the latter, Montmorency.

The Hearts or soft-fleshed Sweets include Seneca and Black Tartarian. The Bigarreaus have firm, sweet flesh and some of the best varieties are Windsor (the hardiest), Bing, Napoleon and Schmidt.

The Dukes are hybrids of Sour and Sweet and reflect the qualities of both parents. They are neither as sweet nor as sour but are somewhere between. They are self-sterile and must be cross-pollinated by some Sweet or Sour variety. If you have Sweets and Sours you will probably not bother with Dukes.

GLOSSARY OF TERMS

Bark ringing. The clean removal of a partial ring of bark just before or during blossom time with the object of inducing fruitfulness. The effect is greater if the rings overlap as shown in Fig. 9, but overlapping is risky and can easily be overdone.

Bending. *Defined page* 49. *See Fig.* 10.

Cion. This is the bud or graft which is budded or grafted into the rootstock and forms the head.

Clon. *Defined pages* 11, 12.

Lateral. *Defined page* 38.

Leader. *Defined page* 37.

Rootstock. *Defined page* 1.

Spur. *Defined page* 38.

Thinning (of branches). *Defined page* 38.

Tip depressing. *Defined page* 49. *See Fig.* 10.

Tipping. *Defined page* 37.

Twisting. *Defined page* 49. *See Fig.* 10.

General Index

Index of Plant Names

A CATALOGUE OF SELECTED DOVER BOOKS
IN ALL FIELDS OF INTEREST

A CATALOGUE OF SELECTED DOVER BOOKS
IN ALL FIELDS OF INTEREST

LEATHER TOOLING AND CARVING, Chris H. Groneman. One of few books concentrating on tooling and carving, with complete instructions and grid designs for 39 projects ranging from bookmarks to bags. 148 illustrations. 111pp. 7⅞ x 10.
23061-9 Pa. $2.50

THE CODEX NUTTALL, A PICTURE MANUSCRIPT FROM ANCIENT MEXICO, as first edited by Zelia Nuttall. Only inexpensive edition, in full color, of a pre-Columbian Mexican (Mixtec) book. 88 color plates show kings, gods, heroes, temples, sacrifices. New explanatory, historical introduction by Arthur G. Miller. 96pp. 11⅜ x 8½.
23168-2 Pa. $7.50

AMERICAN PRIMITIVE PAINTING, Jean Lipman. Classic collection of an enduring American tradition. 109 plates, 8 in full color—portraits, landscapes, Biblical and historical scenes, etc., showing family groups, farm life, and so on. 80pp. of lucid text. 8⅜ x 11¼.
22815-0 Pa. $4.00

WILL BRADLEY: HIS GRAPHIC ART, edited by Clarence P. Hornung. Striking collection of work by foremost practitioner of Art Nouveau in America: posters, cover designs, sample pages, advertisements, other illustrations. 97 plates, including 8 in full color and 19 in two colors. 97pp. 9⅜ x 12¼.
20701-3 Pa. $4.00
22120-2 Clothbd. $10.00

THE UNDERGROUND SKETCHBOOK OF JAN FAUST, Jan Faust. 101 bitter, horrifying, black-humorous, penetrating sketches on sex, war, greed, various liberations, etc. Sometimes sexual, but not pornographic. Not for prudish. 101pp. 6½ x 9¼.
22740-5 Pa. $1.50

THE GIBSON GIRL AND HER AMERICA, Charles Dana Gibson. 155 finest drawings of effervescent world of 1900-1910: the Gibson Girl and her loves, amusements, adventures, Mr. Pipp, etc. Selected by E. Gillon; introduction by Henry Pitz. 144pp. 8¼ x 11⅜.
21986-0 Pa. $3.50

STAINED GLASS CRAFT, J.A.F. Divine, G. Blachford. One of the very few books that tell the beginner exactly what he needs to know: planning cuts, making shapes, avoiding design weaknesses, fitting glass, etc. 93 illustrations. 115pp.
22812-6 Pa. $1.50

CREATIVE LITHOGRAPHY AND HOW TO DO IT, Grant Arnold. Lithography as art form: working directly on stone, transfer of drawings, lithotint, mezzotint, color printing; also metal plates. Detailed, thorough. 27 illustrations. 214pp.
21208-4 Pa. $3.00

DESIGN MOTIFS OF ANCIENT MEXICO, Jorge Enciso. Vigorous, powerful ceramic stamp impressions — Maya, Aztec, Toltec, Olmec. Serpents, gods, priests, dancers, etc. 153pp. 6⅛ x 9¼.
20084-1 Pa. $2.50

AMERICAN INDIAN DESIGN AND DECORATION, Leroy Appleton. Full text, plus more than 700 precise drawings of Inca, Maya, Aztec, Pueblo, Plains, NW Coast basketry, sculpture, painting, pottery, sand paintings, metal, etc. 4 plates in color. 279pp. 8⅜ x 11¼.
22704-9 Pa. $4.50

CHINESE LATTICE DESIGNS, Daniel S. Dye. Incredibly beautiful geometric designs: circles, voluted, simple dissections, etc. Inexhaustible source of ideas, motifs. 1239 illustrations. 469pp. 6⅛ x 9¼.
23096-1 Pa. $5.00

JAPANESE DESIGN MOTIFS, Matsuya Co. Mon, or heraldic designs. Over 4000 typical, beautiful designs: birds, animals, flowers, swords, fans, geometric; all beautifully stylized. 213pp. 11⅜ x 8¼.
22874-6 Pa. $5.00

PERSPECTIVE, Jan Vredeman de Vries. 73 perspective plates from 1604 edition; buildings, townscapes, stairways, fantastic scenes. Remarkable for beauty, surrealistic atmosphere; real eye-catchers. Introduction by Adolf Placzek. 74pp. 11⅜ x 8¼.
20186-4 Pa. $2.75

EARLY AMERICAN DESIGN MOTIFS, Suzanne E. Chapman. 497 motifs, designs, from painting on wood, ceramics, appliqué, glassware, samplers, metal work, etc. Florals, landscapes, birds and animals, geometrics, letters, etc. Inexhaustible. Enlarged edition. 138pp. 8⅜ x 11¼.
22985-8 Pa. $3.50
23084-8 Clothbd. $7.95

VICTORIAN STENCILS FOR DESIGN AND DECORATION, edited by E.V. Gillon, Jr. 113 wonderful ornate Victorian pieces from German sources; florals, geometrics; borders, corner pieces; bird motifs, etc. 64pp. 9⅜ x 12¼.
21995-X Pa. $2.75

ART NOUVEAU: AN ANTHOLOGY OF DESIGN AND ILLUSTRATION FROM THE STUDIO, edited by E.V. Gillon, Jr. Graphic arts: book jackets, posters, engravings, illustrations, decorations; Crane, Beardsley, Bradley and many others. Inexhaustible. 92pp. 8⅛ x 11.
22388-4 Pa. $2.50

ORIGINAL ART DECO DESIGNS, William Rowe. First-rate, highly imaginative modern Art Deco frames, borders, compositions, alphabets, florals, insectals, Wurlitzer-types, etc. Much finest modern Art Deco. 80 plates, 8 in color. 8⅜ x 11¼.
22567-4 Pa. $3.00

HANDBOOK OF DESIGNS AND DEVICES, Clarence P. Hornung. Over 1800 basic geometric designs based on circle, triangle, square, scroll, cross, etc. Largest such collection in existence. 261pp.
20125-2 Pa. $2.50

150 MASTERPIECES OF DRAWING, edited by Anthony Toney. 150 plates, early 15th century to end of 18th century; Rembrandt, Michelangelo, Dürer, Fragonard, Watteau, Wouwerman, many others. 150pp. 8⅜ x 11¼. 21032-4 Pa. $3.50

THE GOLDEN AGE OF THE POSTER, Hayward and Blanche Cirker. 70 extraordinary posters in full colors, from Maîtres de l'Affiche, Mucha, Lautrec, Bradley, Cheret, Beardsley, many others. 9⅜ x 12¼. 22753-7 Pa. $4.95
21718-3 Clothbd. $7.95

SIMPLICISSIMUS, selection, translations and text by Stanley Appelbaum. 180 satirical drawings, 16 in full color, from the famous German weekly magazine in the years 1896 to 1926. 24 artists included: Grosz, Kley, Pascin, Kubin, Kollwitz, plus Heine, Thöny, Bruno Paul, others. 172pp. 8½ x 12¼. 23098-8 Pa. $5.00
23099-6 Clothbd. $10.00

THE EARLY WORK OF AUBREY BEARDSLEY, Aubrey Beardsley. 157 plates, 2 in color: Manon Lescaut, Madame Bovary, Morte d'Arthur, Salome, other. Introduction by H. Marillier. 175pp. 8½ x 11. 21816-3 Pa. $3.50

THE LATER WORK OF AUBREY BEARDSLEY, Aubrey Beardsley. Exotic masterpieces of full maturity: Venus and Tannhäuser, Lysistrata, Rape of the Lock, Volpone, Savoy material, etc. 174 plates, 2 in color. 176pp. 8½ x 11. 21817-1 Pa. $4.00

DRAWINGS OF WILLIAM BLAKE, William Blake. 92 plates from Book of Job, Divine Comedy, Paradise Lost, visionary heads, mythological figures, Laocoön, etc. Selection, introduction, commentary by Sir Geoffrey Keynes. 178pp. 8½ x 11. 22303-5 Pa. $3.50

LONDON: A PILGRIMAGE, Gustave Doré, Blanchard Jerrold. Squalor, riches, misery, beauty of mid-Victorian metropolis; 55 wonderful plates, 125 other illustrations, full social, cultural text by Jerrold. 191pp. of text. 8⅛ x 11. 22306-X Pa. $5.00

THE COMPLETE WOODCUTS OF ALBRECHT DÜRER, edited by Dr. W. Kurth. 346 in all: Old Testament, St. Jerome, Passion, Life of Virgin, Apocalypse, many others. Introduction by Campbell Dodgson. 285pp. 8½ x 12¼. 21097-9 Pa. $6.00

THE DISASTERS OF WAR, Francisco Goya. 83 etchings record horrors of Napoleonic wars in Spain and war in general. Reprint of 1st edition, plus 3 additional plates. Introduction by Philip Hofer. 97pp. 9⅜ x 8¼. 21872-4 Pa. $3.00

ENGRAVINGS OF HOGARTH, William Hogarth. 101 of Hogarth's greatest works: Rake's Progress, Harlot's Progress, Illustrations for Hudibras, Midnight Modern Conversation, Before and After, Beer Street and Gin Lane, many more. Full commentary. 256pp. 11 x 14. 22479-1 Pa. $7.00
23023-6 Clothbd. $13.50

PRIMITIVE ART, Franz Boas. Great anthropologist on ceramics, textiles, wood, stone, metal, etc.; patterns, technology, symbols, styles. All areas, but fullest on Northwest Coast Indians. 350 illustrations. 378pp. 20025-6 Pa. $3.50

MOTHER GOOSE'S MELODIES. Facsimile of fabulously rare Munroe and Francis "copyright 1833" Boston edition. Familiar and unusual rhymes, wonderful old woodcut illustrations. Edited by E.F. Bleiler. 128pp. 4½ x 6⅜. 22577-1 Pa. $1.00

MOTHER GOOSE IN HIEROGLYPHICS. Favorite nursery rhymes presented in rebus form for children. Fascinating 1849 edition reproduced in toto, with key. Introduction by E.F. Bleiler. About 400 woodcuts. 64pp. 6⅞ x 5¼. 20745-5 Pa. $1.00

PETER PIPER'S PRACTICAL PRINCIPLES OF PLAIN & PERFECT PRONUNCIATION. Alliterative jingles and tongue-twisters. Reproduction in full of 1830 first American edition. 25 spirited woodcuts. 32pp. 4½ x 6⅜. 22560-7 Pa. $1.00

MARMADUKE MULTIPLY'S MERRY METHOD OF MAKING MINOR MATHEMATICIANS. Fellow to Peter Piper, it teaches multiplication table by catchy rhymes and woodcuts. 1841 Munroe & Francis edition. Edited by E.F. Bleiler. 103pp. 4⅝ x 6.
22773-1 Pa. $1.25
20171-6 Clothbd. $3.00

THE NIGHT BEFORE CHRISTMAS, Clement Moore. Full text, and woodcuts from original 1848 book. Also critical, historical material. 19 illustrations. 40pp. 4⅝ x 6. 22797-9 Pa. $1.00

THE KING OF THE GOLDEN RIVER, John Ruskin. Victorian children's classic of three brothers, their attempts to reach the Golden River, what becomes of them. Facsimile of original 1889 edition. 22 illustrations. 56pp. 4⅝ x 6⅜.
20066-3 Pa. $1.25

DREAMS OF THE RAREBIT FIEND, Winsor McCay. Pioneer cartoon strip, unexcelled for beauty, imagination, in 60 full sequences. Incredible technical virtuosity, wonderful visual wit. Historical introduction. 62pp. 8⅜ x 11¼. 21347-1 Pa. $2.50

THE KATZENJAMMER KIDS, Rudolf Dirks. In full color, 14 strips from 1906-7; full of imagination, characteristic humor. Classic of great historical importance. Introduction by August Derleth. 32pp. 9¼ x 12¼. 23005-8 Pa. $2.00

LITTLE ORPHAN ANNIE AND LITTLE ORPHAN ANNIE IN COSMIC CITY, Harold Gray. Two great sequences from the early strips: our curly-haired heroine defends the Warbucks' financial empire and, then, takes on meanie Phineas P. Pinchpenny. Leapin' lizards! 178pp. 6⅛ x 8⅜. 23107-0 Pa. $2.00

WHEN A FELLER NEEDS A FRIEND, Clare Briggs. 122 cartoons by one of the greatest newspaper cartoonists of the early 20th century — about growing up, making a living, family life, daily frustrations and occasional triumphs. 121pp. 8½ x 9½.
23148-8 Pa. $2.50

THE BEST OF GLUYAS WILLIAMS. 100 drawings by one of America's finest cartoonists: The Day a Cake of Ivory Soap Sank at Proctor & Gamble's, At the Life Insurance Agents' Banquet, and many other gems from the 20's and 30's. 118pp. 8⅜ x 11¼. 22737-5 Pa. $2.50

THE BEST DR. THORNDYKE DETECTIVE STORIES, R. Austin Freeman. The Case of Oscar Brodski, The Moabite Cipher, and 5 other favorites featuring the great scientific detective, plus his long-believed-lost first adventure — 31 New Inn — reprinted here for the first time. Edited by E.F. Bleiler. USO 20388-3 Pa. $3.00

BEST "THINKING MACHINE" DETECTIVE STORIES, Jacques Futrelle. The Problem of Cell 13 and 11 other stories about Prof. Augustus S.F.X. Van Dusen, including two "lost" stories. First reprinting of several. Edited by E.F. Bleiler. 241pp. 20537-1 Pa. $3.00

UNCLE SILAS, J. Sheridan LeFanu. Victorian Gothic mystery novel, considered by many best of period, even better than Collins or Dickens. Wonderful psychological terror. Introduction by Frederick Shroyer. 436pp. 21715-9 Pa. $4.00

BEST DR. POGGIOLI DETECTIVE STORIES, T.S. Stribling. 15 best stories from EQMM and The Saint offer new adventures in Mexico, Florida, Tennessee hills as Poggioli unravels mysteries and combats Count Jalacki. 217pp. 23227-1 Pa. $3.00

EIGHT DIME NOVELS, selected with an introduction by E.F. Bleiler. Adventures of Old King Brady, Frank James, Nick Carter, Deadwood Dick, Buffalo Bill, The Steam Man, Frank Merriwell, and Horatio Alger — 1877 to 1905. Important, entertaining popular literature in facsimile reprint, with original covers. 190pp. 9 x 12. 22975-0 Pa. $3.50

ALICE'S ADVENTURES UNDER GROUND, Lewis Carroll. Facsimile of ms. Carroll gave Alice Liddell in 1864. Different in many ways from final Alice. Handlettered, illustrated by Carroll. Introduction by Martin Gardner. 128pp. 21482-6 Pa. $1.50

ALICE IN WONDERLAND COLORING BOOK, Lewis Carroll. Pictures by John Tenniel. Large-size versions of the famous illustrations of Alice, Cheshire Cat, Mad Hatter and all the others, waiting for your crayons. Abridged text. 36 illustrations. 64pp. 8¼ x 11. 22853-3 Pa. $1.50

AVENTURES D'ALICE AU PAYS DES MERVEILLES, Lewis Carroll. Bué's translation of "Alice" into French, supervised by Carroll himself. Novel way to learn language. (No English text.) 42 Tenniel illustrations. 196pp. 22836-3 Pa. $2.50

MYTHS AND FOLK TALES OF IRELAND, Jeremiah Curtin. 11 stories that are Irish versions of European fairy tales and 9 stories from the Fenian cycle — 20 tales of legend and magic that comprise an essential work in the history of folklore. 256pp. 22430-9 Pa. $3.00

EAST O' THE SUN AND WEST O' THE MOON, George W. Dasent. Only full edition of favorite, wonderful Norwegian fairytales — Why the Sea is Salt, Boots and the Troll, etc. — with 77 illustrations by Kittelsen & Werenskiöld. 418pp. 22521-6 Pa. $4.00

PERRAULT'S FAIRY TALES, Charles Perrault and Gustave Doré. Original versions of Cinderella, Sleeping Beauty, Little Red Riding Hood, etc. in best translation, with 34 wonderful illustrations by Gustave Doré. 117pp. 8⅛ x 11. 22311-6 Pa. $2.50

EARLY NEW ENGLAND GRAVESTONE RUBBINGS, Edmund V. Gillon, Jr. 43 photographs, 226 rubbings show heavily symbolic, macabre, sometimes humorous primitive American art. Up to early 19th century. 207pp. 8⅜ x 11¼.
21380-3 Pa. $4.00

L.J.M. DAGUERRE: THE HISTORY OF THE DIORAMA AND THE DAGUERREOTYPE, Helmut and Alison Gernsheim. Definitive account. Early history, life and work of Daguerre; discovery of daguerreotype process; diffusion abroad; other early photography. 124 illustrations. 226pp. 6⅙ x 9¼.
22290-X Pa. $4.00

PHOTOGRAPHY AND THE AMERICAN SCENE, Robert Taft. The basic book on American photography as art, recording form, 1839-1889. Development, influence on society, great photographers, types (portraits, war, frontier, etc.), whatever else needed. Inexhaustible. Illustrated with 322 early photos, daguerreotypes, tintypes, stereo slides, etc. 546pp. 6⅛ x 9¼.
21201-7 Pa. $5.95

PHOTOGRAPHIC SKETCHBOOK OF THE CIVIL WAR, Alexander Gardner. Reproduction of 1866 volume with 100 on-the-field photographs: Manassas, Lincoln on battlefield, slave pens, etc. Introduction by E.F. Bleiler. 224pp. 10¾ x 9.
22731-6 Pa. $5.00

THE MOVIES: A PICTURE QUIZ BOOK, Stanley Appelbaum & Hayward Cirker. Match stars with their movies, name actors and actresses, test your movie skill with 241 stills from 236 great movies, 1902-1959. Indexes of performers and films. 128pp. 8⅜ x 9¼.
20222-4 Pa. $2.50

THE TALKIES, Richard Griffith. Anthology of features, articles from Photoplay, 1928-1940, reproduced complete. Stars, famous movies, technical features, fabulous ads, etc.; Garbo, Chaplin, King Kong, Lubitsch, etc. 4 color plates, scores of illustrations. 327pp. 8⅜ x 11¼.
22762-6 Pa. $6.95

THE MOVIE MUSICAL FROM VITAPHONE TO "42ND STREET," edited by Miles Kreuger. Relive the rise of the movie musical as reported in the pages of Photoplay magazine (1926-1933): every movie review, cast list, ad, and record review; every significant feature article, production still, biography, forecast, and gossip story. Profusely illustrated. 367pp. 8⅜ x 11¼.
23154-2 Pa. $6.95

JOHANN SEBASTIAN BACH, Philipp Spitta. Great classic of biography, musical commentary, with hundreds of pieces analyzed. Also good for Bach's contemporaries. 450 musical examples. Total of 1799pp.
EUK 22278-0, 22279-9 Clothbd., Two vol. set $25.00

BEETHOVEN AND HIS NINE SYMPHONIES, Sir George Grove. Thorough history, analysis, commentary on symphonies and some related pieces. For either beginner or advanced student. 436 musical passages. 407pp.
20334-4 Pa. $4.00

MOZART AND HIS PIANO CONCERTOS, Cuthbert Girdlestone. The only full-length study. Detailed analyses of all 21 concertos, sources; 417 musical examples. 509pp.
21271-8 Pa. $4.50

THE FITZWILLIAM VIRGINAL BOOK, edited by J. Fuller Maitland, W.B. Squire. Famous early 17th century collection of keyboard music, 300 works by Morley, Byrd, Bull, Gibbons, etc. Modern notation. Total of 938pp. 8⅜ x 11.
ECE 21068-5, 21069-3 Pa., Two vol. set $14.00

COMPLETE STRING QUARTETS, Wolfgang A. Mozart. Breitkopf and Härtel edition. All 23 string quartets plus alternate slow movement to K156. Study score. 277pp. 9⅜ x 12¼.
22372-8 Pa. $6.00

COMPLETE SONG CYCLES, Franz Schubert. Complete piano, vocal music of Die Schöne Müllerin, Die Winterreise, Schwanengesang. Also Drinker English singing translations. Breitkopf and Härtel edition. 217pp. 9⅜ x 12¼.
22649-2 Pa. $4.50

THE COMPLETE PRELUDES AND ETUDES FOR PIANOFORTE SOLO, Alexander Scriabin. All the preludes and etudes including many perfectly spun miniatures. Edited by K.N. Igumnov and Y.I. Mil'shteyn. 250pp. 9 x 12.
22919-X Pa. $5.00

TRISTAN UND ISOLDE, Richard Wagner. Full orchestral score with complete instrumentation. Do not confuse with piano reduction. Commentary by Felix Mottl, great Wagnerian conductor and scholar. Study score. 655pp. 8⅛ x 11.
22915-7 Pa. $10.00

FAVORITE SONGS OF THE NINETIES, ed. Robert Fremont. Full reproduction, including covers, of 88 favorites: Ta-Ra-Ra-Boom-De-Aye, The Band Played On, Bird in a Gilded Cage, Under the Bamboo Tree, After the Ball, etc. 401pp. 9 x 12.
EBE 21536-9 Pa. $6.95

SOUSA'S GREAT MARCHES IN PIANO TRANSCRIPTION: ORIGINAL SHEET MUSIC OF 23 WORKS, John Philip Sousa. Selected by Lester S. Levy. Playing edition includes: The Stars and Stripes Forever, The Thunderer, The Gladiator, King Cotton, Washington Post, much more. 24 illustrations. 111pp. 9 x 12.
USO 23132-1 Pa. $3.50

CLASSIC PIANO RAGS, selected with an introduction by Rudi Blesh. Best ragtime music (1897-1922) by Scott Joplin, James Scott, Joseph F. Lamb, Tom Turpin, 9 others. Printed from best original sheet music, plus covers. 364pp. 9 x 12.
EBE 20469-3 Pa. $6.95

ANALYSIS OF CHINESE CHARACTERS, C.D. Wilder, J.H. Ingram. 1000 most important characters analyzed according to primitives, phonetics, historical development. Traditional method offers mnemonic aid to beginner, intermediate student of Chinese, Japanese. 365pp.
23045-7 Pa. $4.00

MODERN CHINESE: A BASIC COURSE, Faculty of Peking University. Self study, classroom course in modern Mandarin. Records contain phonetics, vocabulary, sentences, lessons. 249 page book contains all recorded text, translations, grammar, vocabulary, exercises. Best course on market. 3 12" 33⅓ monaural records, book, album.
98832-5 Set $12.50

MANUAL OF THE TREES OF NORTH AMERICA, Charles S. Sargent. The basic survey of every native tree and tree-like shrub, 717 species in all. Extremely full descriptions, information on habitat, growth, locales, economics, etc. Necessary to every serious tree lover. Over 100 finding keys. 783 illustrations. Total of 986pp.
20277-1, 20278-X Pa., Two vol. set $8.00

BIRDS OF THE NEW YORK AREA, John Bull. Indispensable guide to more than 400 species within a hundred-mile radius of Manhattan. Information on range, status, breeding, migration, distribution trends, etc. Foreword by Roger Tory Peterson. 17 drawings; maps. 540pp. 23222-0 Pa. $6.00

THE SEA-BEACH AT EBB-TIDE, Augusta Foote Arnold. Identify hundreds of marine plants and animals: algae, seaweeds, squids, crabs, corals, etc. Descriptions cover food, life cycle, size, shape, habitat. Over 600 drawings. 490pp.
21949-6 Pa. $5.00

THE MOTH BOOK, William J. Holland. Identify more than 2,000 moths of North America. General information, precise species descriptions. 623 illustrations plus 48 color plates show almost all species, full size. 1968 edition. Still the basic book. Total of 551pp. 6½ x 9¼. 21948-8 Pa. $6.00

AN INTRODUCTION TO THE REPTILES AND AMPHIBIANS OF THE UNITED STATES, Percy A. Morris. All lizards, crocodiles, turtles, snakes, toads, frogs; life history, identification, habits, suitability as pets, etc. Non-technical, but sound and broad. 130 photos. 253pp. 22982-3 Pa. $3.00

OLD NEW YORK IN EARLY PHOTOGRAPHS, edited by Mary Black. Your only chance to see New York City as it was 1853-1906, through 196 wonderful photographs from N.Y. Historical Society. Great Blizzard, Lincoln's funeral procession, great buildings. 228pp. 9 x 12. 22907-6 Pa. $6.00

THE AMERICAN REVOLUTION, A PICTURE SOURCEBOOK, John Grafton. Wonderful Bicentennial picture source, with 411 illustrations (contemporary and 19th century) showing battles, personalities, maps, events, flags, posters, soldier's life, ships, etc. all captioned and explained. A wonderful browsing book, supplement to other historical reading. 160pp. 9 x 12. 23226-3 Pa. $4.00

PERSONAL NARRATIVE OF A PILGRIMAGE TO AL-MADINAH AND MECCAH, Richard Burton. Great travel classic by remarkably colorful personality. Burton, disguised as a Moroccan, visited sacred shrines of Islam, narrowly escaping death. Wonderful observations of Islamic life, customs, personalities. 47 illustrations. Total of 959pp. 21217-3, 21218-1 Pa., Two vol. set $10.00

INCIDENTS OF TRAVEL IN CENTRAL AMERICA, CHIAPAS, AND YUCATAN, John L. Stephens. Almost single-handed discovery of Maya culture; exploration of ruined cities, monuments, temples; customs of Indians. 115 drawings. 892pp.
22404-X, 22405-8 Pa., Two vol. set $8.00

CONSTRUCTION OF AMERICAN FURNITURE TREASURES, Lester Margon. 344 detail drawings, complete text on constructing exact reproductions of 38 early American masterpieces: Hepplewhite sideboard, Duncan Phyfe drop-leaf table, mantel clock, gate-leg dining table, Pa. German cupboard, more. 38 plates. 54 photographs. 168pp. 8⅜ x 11¼.   23056-2 Pa. $4.00

JEWELRY MAKING AND DESIGN, Augustus F. Rose, Antonio Cirino. Professional secrets revealed in thorough, practical guide: tools, materials, processes; rings, brooches, chains, cast pieces, enamelling, setting stones, etc. Do not confuse with skimpy introductions: beginner can use, professional can learn from it. Over 200 illustrations. 306pp.   21750-7 Pa. $3.00

METALWORK AND ENAMELLING, Herbert Maryon. Generally conceded best all-around book. Countless trade secrets: materials, tools, soldering, filigree, setting, inlay, niello, repoussé, casting, polishing, etc. For beginner or expert. Author was foremost British expert. 330 illustrations. 335pp.   22702-2 Pa. $3.50

WEAVING WITH FOOT-POWER LOOMS, Edward F. Worst. Setting up a loom, beginning to weave, constructing equipment, using dyes, more, plus over 285 drafts of traditional patterns including Colonial and Swedish weaves. More than 200 other figures. For beginning and advanced. 275pp. 8¾ x 6⅜.   23064-3 Pa. $4.00

WEAVING A NAVAJO BLANKET, Gladys A. Reichard. Foremost anthropologist studied under Navajo women, reveals every step in process from wool, dyeing, spinning, setting up loom, designing, weaving. Much history, symbolism. With this book you could make one yourself. 97 illustrations. 222pp.   22992-0 Pa. $3.00

NATURAL DYES AND HOME DYEING, Rita J. Adrosko. Use natural ingredients: bark, flowers, leaves, lichens, insects etc. Over 135 specific recipes from historical sources for cotton, wool, other fabrics. Genuine premodern handicrafts. 12 illustrations. 160pp.   22688-3 Pa. $2.00

THE HAND DECORATION OF FABRICS, Francis J. Kafka. Outstanding, profusely illustrated guide to stenciling, batik, block printing, tie dyeing, freehand painting, silk screen printing, and novelty decoration. 356 illustrations. 198pp. 6 x 9.
21401-X Pa. $3.00

THOMAS NAST: CARTOONS AND ILLUSTRATIONS, with text by Thomas Nast St. Hill. Father of American political cartooning. Cartoons that destroyed Tweed Ring; inflation, free love, church and state; original Republican elephant and Democratic donkey; Santa Claus; more. 117 illustrations. 146pp. 9 x 12.
22983-1 Pa. $4.00
23067-8 Clothbd. $8.50

FREDERIC REMINGTON: 173 DRAWINGS AND ILLUSTRATIONS. Most famous of the Western artists, most responsible for our myths about the American West in its untamed days. Complete reprinting of *Drawings of Frederic Remington* (1897), plus other selections. 4 additional drawings in color on covers. 140pp. 9 x 12.
20714-5 Pa. $3.95

How to Solve Chess Problems, Kenneth S. Howard. Practical suggestions on problem solving for very beginners. 58 two-move problems, 46 3-movers, 8 4-movers for practice, plus hints. 171pp.   20748-X Pa. $2.00

A Guide to Fairy Chess, Anthony Dickins. 3-D chess, 4-D chess, chess on a cylindrical board, reflecting pieces that bounce off edges, cooperative chess, retrograde chess, maximummers, much more. Most based on work of great Dawson. Full handbook, 100 problems. 66pp. 7⅞ x 10¾.   22687-5 Pa. $2.00

Win at Backgammon, Millard Hopper. Best opening moves, running game, blocking game, back game, tables of odds, etc. Hopper makes the game clear enough for anyone to play, and win. 43 diagrams. 111pp.   22894-0 Pa. $1.50

Bidding a Bridge Hand, Terence Reese. Master player "thinks out loud" the binding of 75 hands that defy point count systems. Organized by bidding problem—no-fit situations, overbidding, underbidding, cueing your defense, etc. 254pp.   EBE 22830-4 Pa. $2.50

The Precision Bidding System in Bridge, C.C. Wei, edited by Alan Truscott. Inventor of precision bidding presents average hands and hands from actual play, including games from 1969 Bermuda Bowl where system emerged. 114 exercises. 116pp.   21171-1 Pa. $1.75

Learn Magic, Henry Hay. 20 simple, easy-to-follow lessons on magic for the new magician: illusions, card tricks, silks, sleights of hand, coin manipulations, escapes, and more —all with a minimum amount of equipment. Final chapter explains the great stage illusions. 92 illustrations. 285pp.   21238-6 Pa. $2.95

The New Magician's Manual, Walter B. Gibson. Step-by-step instructions and clear illustrations guide the novice in mastering 36 tricks; much equipment supplied on 16 pages of cut-out materials. 36 additional tricks. 64 illustrations. 159pp. 6⅝ x 10.   23113-5 Pa. $3.00

Professional Magic for Amateurs, Walter B. Gibson. 50 easy, effective tricks used by professionals —cards, string, tumblers, handkerchiefs, mental magic, etc. 63 illustrations. 223pp.   23012-0 Pa. $2.50

Card Manipulations, Jean Hugard. Very rich collection of manipulations; has taught thousands of fine magicians tricks that are really workable, eye-catching. Easily followed, serious work. Over 200 illustrations. 163pp. 20539-8 Pa. $2.00

Abbott's Encyclopedia of Rope Tricks for Magicians, Stewart James. Complete reference book for amateur and professional magicians containing more than 150 tricks involving knots, penetrations, cut and restored rope, etc. 510 illustrations. Reprint of 3rd edition. 400pp.   23206-9 Pa. $3.50

The Secrets of Houdini, J.C. Cannell. Classic study of Houdini's incredible magic, exposing closely-kept professional secrets and revealing, in general terms, the whole art of stage magic. 67 illustrations. 279pp.   22913-0 Pa. $2.50

THE MAGIC MOVING PICTURE BOOK, Bliss, Sands & Co. The pictures in this book move! Volcanoes erupt, a house burns, a serpentine dancer wiggles her way through a number. By using a specially ruled acetate screen provided, you can obtain these and 15 other startling effects. Originally "The Motograph Moving Picture Book." 32pp. 8¼ x 11.   23224-7 Pa. $1.75

STRING FIGURES AND HOW TO MAKE THEM, Caroline F. Jayne. Fullest, clearest instructions on string figures from around world: Eskimo, Navajo, Lapp, Europe, more. Cats cradle, moving spear, lightning, stars. Introduction by A.C. Haddon. 950 illustrations. 407pp.   20152-X Pa. $3.00

PAPER FOLDING FOR BEGINNERS, William D. Murray and Francis J. Rigney. Clearest book on market for making origami sail boats, roosters, frogs that move legs, cups, bonbon boxes. 40 projects. More than 275 illustrations. Photographs. 94pp.   20713-7 Pa. $1.25

INDIAN SIGN LANGUAGE, William Tomkins. Over 525 signs developed by Sioux, Blackfoot, Cheyenne, Arapahoe and other tribes. Written instructions and diagrams: how to make words, construct sentences. Also 290 pictographs of Sioux and Ojibway tribes. 111pp. 6⅛ x 9¼.   22029-X Pa. $1.50

BOOMERANGS: HOW TO MAKE AND THROW THEM, Bernard S. Mason. Easy to make and throw, dozens of designs: cross-stick, pinwheel, boomabird, tumblestick, Australian curved stick boomerang. Complete throwing instructions. All safe. 99pp.   23028-7 Pa. $1.50

25 KITES THAT FLY, Leslie Hunt. Full, easy to follow instructions for kites made from inexpensive materials. Many novelties. Reeling, raising, designing your own. 70 illustrations. 110pp.   22550-X Pa. $1.25

TRICKS AND GAMES ON THE POOL TABLE, Fred Herrmann. 79 tricks and games, some solitaires, some for 2 or more players, some competitive; mystifying shots and throws, unusual carom, tricks involving cork, coins, a hat, more. 77 figures. 95pp.   21814-7 Pa. $1.25

WOODCRAFT AND CAMPING, Bernard S. Mason. How to make a quick emergency shelter, select woods that will burn immediately, make do with limited supplies, etc. Also making many things out of wood, rawhide, bark, at camp. Formerly titled Woodcraft. 295 illustrations. 580pp.   21951-8 Pa. $4.00

AN INTRODUCTION TO CHESS MOVES AND TACTICS SIMPLY EXPLAINED, Leonard Barden. Informal intermediate introduction: reasons for moves, tactics, openings, traps, positional play, endgame. Isolates patterns. 102pp. USO 21210-6 Pa. $1.35

LASKER'S MANUAL OF CHESS, Dr. Emanuel Lasker. Great world champion offers very thorough coverage of all aspects of chess. Combinations, position play, openings, endgame, aesthetics of chess, philosophy of struggle, much more. Filled with analyzed games. 390pp.   20640-8 Pa. $3.50

SLEEPING BEAUTY, illustrated by Arthur Rackham. Perhaps the fullest, most delightful version ever, told by C.S. Evans. Rackham's best work. 49 illustrations. 110pp. 7⅞ x 10¾. 22756-1 Pa. $2.00

THE WONDERFUL WIZARD OF OZ, L. Frank Baum. Facsimile in full color of America's finest children's classic. Introduction by Martin Gardner. 143 illustrations by W.W. Denslow. 267pp. 20691-2 Pa. $2.50

GOOPS AND HOW TO BE THEM, Gelett Burgess. Classic tongue-in-cheek masquerading as etiquette book. 87 verses, 170 cartoons as Goops demonstrate virtues of table manners, neatness, courtesy, more. 88pp. 6½ x 9¼. 22233-0 Pa. $1.50

THE BROWNIES, THEIR BOOK, Palmer Cox. Small as mice, cunning as foxes, exuberant, mischievous, Brownies go to zoo, toy shop, seashore, circus, more. 24 verse adventures. 266 illustrations. 144pp. 6⅝ x 9¼. 21265-3 Pa. $1.75

BILLY WHISKERS: THE AUTOBIOGRAPHY OF A GOAT, Frances Trego Montgomery. Escapades of that rambunctious goat. Favorite from turn of the century America. 24 illustrations. 259pp. 22345-0 Pa. $2.75

THE ROCKET BOOK, Peter Newell. Fritz, janitor's kid, sets off rocket in basement of apartment house; an ingenious hole punched through every page traces course of rocket. 22 duotone drawings, verses. 48pp. 6⅞ x 8⅜. 22044-3 Pa. $1.50

PECK'S BAD BOY AND HIS PA, George W. Peck. Complete double-volume of great American childhood classic. Hennery's ingenious pranks against outraged pomposity of pa and the grocery man. 97 illustrations. Introduction by E.F. Bleiler. 347pp. 20497-9 Pa. $2.50

THE TALE OF PETER RABBIT, Beatrix Potter. The inimitable Peter's terrifying adventure in Mr. McGregor's garden, with all 27 wonderful, full-color Potter illustrations. 55pp. 4¼ x 5½. USO 22827-4 Pa. $1.00

THE TALE OF MRS. TIGGY-WINKLE, Beatrix Potter. Your child will love this story about a very special hedgehog and all 27 wonderful, full-color Potter illustrations. 57pp. 4¼ x 5½. USO 20546-0 Pa. $1.00

THE TALE OF BENJAMIN BUNNY, Beatrix Potter. Peter Rabbit's cousin coaxes him back into Mr. McGregor's garden for a whole new set of adventures. A favorite with children. All 27 full-color illustrations. 59pp. 4¼ x 5½. USO 21102-9 Pa. $1.00

THE MERRY ADVENTURES OF ROBIN HOOD, Howard Pyle. Facsimile of original (1883) edition, finest modern version of English outlaw's adventures. 23 illustrations by Pyle. 296pp. 6½ x 9¼. 22043-5 Pa. $2.75

TWO LITTLE SAVAGES, Ernest Thompson Seton. Adventures of two boys who lived as Indians; explaining Indian ways, woodlore, pioneer methods. 293 illustrations. 286pp. 20985-7 Pa. $3.00

HOUDINI ON MAGIC, Harold Houdini. Edited by Walter Gibson, Morris N. Young. How he escaped; exposés of fake spiritualists; instructions for eye-catching tricks; other fascinating material by and about greatest magician. 155 illustrations. 280pp.   20384-0 Pa. $2.50

HANDBOOK OF THE NUTRITIONAL CONTENTS OF FOOD, U.S. Dept. of Agriculture. Largest, most detailed source of food nutrition information ever prepared. Two mammoth tables: one measuring nutrients in 100 grams of edible portion; the other, in edible portion of 1 pound as purchased. Originally titled Composition of Foods. 190pp. 9 x 12.   21342-0 Pa. $4.00

COMPLETE GUIDE TO HOME CANNING, PRESERVING AND FREEZING, U.S. Dept. of Agriculture. Seven basic manuals with full instructions for jams and jellies; pickles and relishes; canning fruits, vegetables, meat; freezing anything. Really good recipes, exact instructions for optimal results. Save a fortune in food. 156 illustrations. 214pp. 6⅛ x 9¼.   22911-4 Pa. $2.50

THE BREAD TRAY, Louis P. De Gouy. Nearly every bread the cook could buy or make: bread sticks of Italy, fruit breads of Greece, glazed rolls of Vienna, everything from corn pone to croissants. Over 500 recipes altogether. including buns, rolls, muffins, scones, and more. 463pp.   23000-7 Pa. $3.50

CREATIVE HAMBURGER COOKERY, Louis P. De Gouy. 182 unusual recipes for casseroles, meat loaves and hamburgers that turn inexpensive ground meat into memorable main dishes: Arizona chili burgers, burger tamale pie, burger stew, burger corn loaf, burger wine loaf, and more. 120pp.   23001-5 Pa. $1.75

LONG ISLAND SEAFOOD COOKBOOK, J. George Frederick and Jean Joyce. Probably the best American seafood cookbook. Hundreds of recipes. 40 gourmet sauces, 123 recipes using oysters alone! All varieties of fish and seafood amply represented. 324pp.   22677-8 Pa. $3.00

THE EPICUREAN: A COMPLETE TREATISE OF ANALYTICAL AND PRACTICAL STUDIES IN THE CULINARY ART, Charles Ranhofer. Great modern classic. 3,500 recipes from master chef of Delmonico's, turn-of-the-century America's best restaurant. Also explained, many techniques known only to professional chefs. 775 illustrations. 1183pp. 6⅝ x 10.   22680-8 Clothbd. $17.50

THE AMERICAN WINE COOK BOOK, Ted Hatch. Over 700 recipes: old favorites livened up with wine plus many more: Czech fish soup, quince soup, sauce Perigueux, shrimp shortcake, filets Stroganoff, cordon bleu goulash, jambonneau, wine fruit cake, more. 314pp.   22796-0 Pa. $2.50

DELICIOUS VEGETARIAN COOKING, Ivan Baker. Close to 500 delicious and varied recipes: soups, main course dishes (pea, bean, lentil, cheese, vegetable, pasta, and egg dishes), savories, stews, whole-wheat breads and cakes, more. 168pp.
USO 22834-7 Pa. $1.75

COOKIES FROM MANY LANDS, Josephine Perry. Crullers, oatmeal cookies, chaux au chocolate, English tea cakes, mandel kuchen, Sacher torte, Danish puff pastry, Swedish cookies — a mouth-watering collection of 223 recipes. 157pp.
22832-0 Pa. $2.00

ROSE RECIPES, Eleanour S. Rohde. How to make sauces, jellies, tarts, salads, pot-pourris, sweet bags, pomanders, perfumes from garden roses; all exact recipes. Century old favorites. 95pp.
22957-2 Pa. $1.25

"OSCAR" OF THE WALDORF'S COOKBOOK, Oscar Tschirky. Famous American chef reveals 3455 recipes that made Waldorf great; cream of French, German, American cooking, in all categories. Full instructions, easy home use. 1896 edition. 907pp. 6⅝ x 9⅜.
20790-0 Clothbd. $15.00

JAMS AND JELLIES, May Byron. Over 500 old-time recipes for delicious jams, jellies, marmalades, preserves, and many other items. Probably the largest jam and jelly book in print. Originally titled May Byron's Jam Book. 276pp.
USO 23130-5 Pa. $3.00

MUSHROOM RECIPES, André L. Simon. 110 recipes for everyday and special cooking. Champignons à la grecque, sole bonne femme, chicken liver croustades, more; 9 basic sauces, 13 ways of cooking mushrooms. 54pp.
USO 20913-X Pa. $1.25

FAVORITE SWEDISH RECIPES, edited by Sam Widenfelt. Prepared in Sweden, offers wonderful, clearly explained Swedish dishes: appetizers, meats, pastry and cookies, other categories. Suitable for American kitchen. 90 photos. 157pp.
23156-9 Pa. $2.00

THE BUCKEYE COOKBOOK, Buckeye Publishing Company. Over 1,000 easy-to-follow, traditional recipes from the American Midwest: bread (100 recipes alone), meat, game, jam, candy, cake, ice cream, and many other categories of cooking. 64 illustrations. From 1883 enlarged edition. 416pp.
23218-2 Pa. $4.00

TWENTY-TWO AUTHENTIC BANQUETS FROM INDIA, Robert H. Christie. Complete, easy-to-do recipes for almost 200 authentic Indian dishes assembled in 22 banquets. Arranged by region. Selected from Banquets of the Nations. 192pp.
23200-X Pa. $2.50